6 29 /33/ Haining P.

Checked
21/10/11

Hertfordshire
COUNTY COUNCIL
Community Information

09/08

12 APR 2002

D1587319

Please renew/return this item by the last date shown.

So that your telephone call is charged at local rate,
please call the numbers as set out below:

	From Area codes 01923 or 020:	From the rest of Herts:
Renewals:	01923 471373	01438 737373
Enquiries:	01923 471333	01438 737333
Minicom:	01923 471599	01438 737599

L32   www.hertsdirect.org

The Compleat Birdman

The Compleat Birdman

An Illustrated History of Man-Powered Flight

PETER HAINING

ROBERT HALE LIMITED
LONDON
ST. MARTIN'S PRESS
NEW YORK

© *Peter Haining 1976*
First published in Great Britain 1976
First published in the United States of America 1977

ISBN 0 7091 5758 4

Robert Hale Limited
Clerkenwell House
Clerkenwell Green
London EC1

St. Martin's Press, Inc.
175 Fifth Avenue
New York, N.Y. 10010

Library of Congress Catalog Card Number 76-26718

For
My Mother and Father
—with love

Printed in Great Britain by
Clarke, Doble & Brendon Ltd,
Plymouth

Contents

Illustrations

Acknowledgements

The author would like to extend his thanks to the following, who particularly helped him during the course of writing this book with advice, reference material, photographs and illustrations: the staff of the Library of the Royal Aeronautical Society, London; The Science Museum, The British Museum and The London Library; The British Hang-Gliding Association and the United States Hang-Gliding Association; John W. R. Taylor for help and suggestions, and the admirable aeronautical works of Charles Gibbs-Smith, M. J. B. Davy and Clive Hart. Many of the illustrations in this work are from the author's own collection, and the copying of these was under the supervision of Christopher Scott. Other than the sources already mentioned, pictures were also supplied by the *Scientific American*, MGM and British Lion Pictures, the *Sun*, the *News of the World*, *Illustrated London News*, the *Daily Telegraph*, *Paris-Match*, *Stern*, Fleetway Publications, *Pilot* magazine, The Northrop Institute of Technology, California, The Singer Co., Benson & Hedges Ltd, Conway Picture Library, The British Film Institute, the National Film Archive, Planet News, Camera Press, *Flight International*, Stanley Gibbons Ltd, Keystone Press Ltd and Messrs Faber & Faber. Finally, I must thank my wife, Philippa, who typed the manuscript and assisted me in so many different and important ways.

PETER HAINING

"Who knows perhaps yet but the
world shall see,
Thae glorious days when folk
shall learn to fly."

ANDREW SCOTT (1757–1839)
[Scottish labourer and poet]

[1]

The Birdman Tradition

It was a warm, early autumn morning in the small Essex hamlet of Chigwell Row. The village was little more than a straggle of small cottages and houses lying on the eastern fringe of Epping Forest and most of the residents worked on the land or in the forest itself. Although the sun was well up in the sky on this September morning in 1862, few people had gone to work and there were still quite a number of children who should have been at school, loitering around the community's one shop, a general store. Several dozen of the residents stood in small groups, their conversations light-hearted but muted as they awaited the arrival of George Faux, the village carrier and deliveryman—the man who said that he could fly.

Faux was a tall, well-built farm worker passionately interested in the concept of man-powered flight. He was known as a character, a drinker and—behind his back—as a bit of an eccentric. On many an evening he had held court in the local public house, and others in the district, declaiming his theory of flight. Man would fly up into the heavens soon, he maintained, and under his own power. And he wouldn't need wings or any such devices, he told his audience, just the skill of his arms thrusting through the air in the "special way of birds".

Throughout his life, George—who was now 62—had made an intensive study of birds and was convinced that it was the way they cleaved through the air with the *front edges* of their wings, rather than with the whole surface, that enabled them to fly. He said he could do the same with his own bare arms. George was too big and powerful a man, even at his age, for anyone to laugh in his face—one stranger had, and received a bloodied nose—but the wry smiles which went on when he looked the other way told their own story about the attitude of the Chigwell Row residents to their strange neighbour. When he had perfected his arm stroke, said George, he would show them all by taking off into the heavens.

By September 1862 he believed he was ready to make his great attempt from the roof of the tallest building in the village—appropriately enough, the public house.

Shortly after nine o'clock George came out of his cottage to the cheers of his neighbours and climbed up a ladder, which had previously been made ready, onto the roof. The chatter of the assembled people hushed and all eyes were upon the figure above them. There were a few startled cries from the womenfolk when the carrier began stripping off his clothes—and but for their own intense concentration, the men might well have sent their wives indoors so that they should not see—but the tension now was too strong for that. Down to his underpants, George began to flex his long sunburnt arms and breathe in great gulps of air. After several more minutes of exercise he moved to the guttering of the roof and lowered himself into a crouching position. Taking one more deep breath, he began to wave his arms steadily up and down, holding them out rigidly and pointing the fingers. With a great leap he pushed himself forward.

The crowd gasped, staggered back. Women covered their eyes and strong men felt their throats go dry. Children screamed.

Beating his arms vainly, his eyes a mixture of bewilderment and panic, George Faux plunged straight down onto the dirt path below. For a moment he lay quite still and then a low moan escaped from his lips. With an audible sigh of relief the villagers crowded around the fallen birdman. Eager hands helped him to his feet, and although his face was scratched and his body was bruised, luckily no bones seemed to be broken. To murmurs of sympathy and queries as to whether he was all right, George nodded his head dumbly.

As he slumped on the wooden bench in front of the inn to regain his breath, someone at the back of the crowd—perhaps feeling brave at the temporary indisposition of the giant—called out, "Why did you do it then, George?"

The carrier was silent a minute, as if in thought, and then he retorted simply, "I'm really a good flyer," he said, "but I cannot alight very well."

A ripple of good-natured laughter ran through the crowd, and the publican arrived at that moment with George's clothes which he had recovered from the roof, as well as a pint of ale. George took a huge swig of the ale and stood up to get back into his clothes.

"I am right, you know," he went on to those who were not already walking away, "man will fly like a bird." He stepped into his trousers and added, "I'm not afraid of hurting myself, but I would rather tear my skin than my clothes: the skin will mend itself, but the clothes will not!"

This intrepid but foolhardy birdman was to make several more attempts to fly from roofs, so convinced was he about his theory of flight. In the end it was a broken leg sustained by jumping off the roof of the local squire's house—without his permission—which grounded him for good. His aeronautics were thereafter banned on pain of a week in the local lock-up!

Bizarre though his theory was, George Faux was just one more human being possessed with the desire to fly like a bird —a desire which has driven men of all nations, and all generations, to bravery and endeavour. George was also the man whose story, when I heard it, gave me the idea of writing the history of 'The Compleat Birdman'.

"Every man has an innate inclination to fly," wrote the German novelist and critic E. T. A. Hoffman some one hundred and fifty years ago—an inclination which is as strong today in the space age as it was at the dawn of history. Indeed, ever since he first observed the freedom of birds on the wing, earth-bound man has sought to emulate them—and even though he has now achieved this end with the assistance of machinery, he still has the urge to do so under his own power.

Both history and literature reflect this desire from one period to the next, mirroring the words of the Psalms: "O that I had wings like a dove, for then I would fly away and be at rest." And what a history it is: a pageant of drama and thrills, of so-near success and tragic failure, of public ridicule and personal courage, of humour, pathos and sometimes death.

As the historian Charles H. Gibbs-Smith has noted in *A History of Flying* (1953),

The idea of human flight has engaged the waking and the sleeping thoughts of many men since the beginning of history. For flying has never appeared to its early pioneers—nor to present-day airmen—as merely a method of locomotion, faster or more convenient than travel by land or water. It has always made a powerful appeal to the emotions; an appeal both to the longing for escape and to the desire for power and exhilaration. Some may also see in it the symbol of aspiration.

What first motivated this desire has, naturally, inspired much speculation. Was it early man's search for spiritual as well as physical elevation—in other words a need to get closer to the gods that he worshipped? Or, much more simply, was it promoted by envy—the oldest and most deadly sin of all—of the freedom of birds?

John W. Taylor, another aeronautical expert, has summarized both schools of thought:

> Even on the most mundane level it was natural that the sky should claim much of man's attention, for it was the source of the sunshine, wind and rain that governed his daily comfort and influenced the prosperity of his crops. Whatever the gods that he worshipped, they all dwelt 'up there', for only from the heavens could they be all-seeing and direct the pattern of events upon the earth below.

> To the ancient Greek, it was perfectly natural to credit his gods with the power of flight—for how else could they descend from Mount Olympus? The Greek god Hermes, in particular, is always depicted wearing winged head-dress and sandals; while Swiatowid, a major god of the western Slav peoples, also rode through the sky above his domains. This image of the winged object of worship repeats itself the world over, in the legends and folk stories of many nations; for early man, unable to fly himself, regarded the ability to do so as proof of supernatural powers.

Perhaps, most simply, the desire to fly was a wish on man's part to break out of his natural environment, as M. J. B. Davy has said in his *Interpretative History of Flight* (1948):

> The will to fly was the will to conquer, to overcome all obstacles in the effort to gain control over natural conditions of environment, and it pervaded the mind of man throughout the earliest civilizations.

In these earliest civilizations, man undoubtedly saw himself as imperfect and restricted, but as his reason developed he realized that flight was not just a supernatural achievement —after all it was common in nature—but an accomplishment that, although denied to him, did not transcend any natural law. It was therefore a physical phenomenon—and as he had already proved himself superior to all other living creatures and had built himself transport across both land and sea, he set out on the long trail of speculating how to achieve mastery of the air under his own power, a question which has now engrossed him for several thousand years.

Both Oriental and Western folklore is, as we know, full of tales of aerial locomotion—magic conveyances, witches on broomsticks and all manner of flying men—but though some of the stories are based on fact (as we shall see in later chapters) they were all abortive attempts. However, they did serve one absolutely vital purpose, as M. J. B. Davy has pointed out: "They caused the idea of man-flight to endure during periods when the spirit of conquest was waning."

Charles Gibbs-Smith has reinforced this statement: "Drawn by the curious fascination of flight, prophets arose to foretell the conquest of the air, as well as the blessings and calamities that would come of it."

Robert Burton, in the seventeenth century, saw the challenge of 'conquest' thus: "If the heavens then be penetrable, and no lets, it were not amiss to make wings and fly up; and some new-fangled wits, methinks, should some time or other find out." Samuel Johnson, a century later, was less sure of the 'blessings'; "If all men were virtuous, I should with great alacrity teach them all to fly. But what would be the security of the good, if the bad could at pleasure invade them from the sky?"

William Cowper, at the same time, saw only the 'calamities': "I would make it death for a man to be convicted of flying the moment he could be caught. . . . Historians would load my memory with reproaches of phlegm and stupidity and oppression; but in the meantime the world would go on quietly, and if it enjoyed less liberty, would at least be more secure." (Both Johnson and Cowper had envisaged the dangers of aerial bombardment.)

Such pros and cons were, however, to have no effect on the endeavours of the birdmen—brave and mostly foolish men who took off from high places with feathers on their arms or

B

wings on their backs and plunged down to serious injury or even death.

Clive Hart tells us in *The Dream of Flight* (1972) how it must have been:

> For the primitive aeronauts a great deal of daring was essential: not only physical daring to risk one's neck with flimsy and untried machinery, but also psychological daring, to step out of one's normal element and act in apparent defiance of all the dictates of nature. For even flight conceived as an organic relationship with the natural world was a hazardous departure from the established order. The old adage 'if God had meant man to fly, He'd have given him wings' was often taken very seriously indeed, and many conventional moralists drew comfort from the repeated stories of failure. Man's physical tendency to fall to the ground was seen by some as an observable correspondence with his fallen moral nature, so that attempts to fly might be said, in a sense, to be almost blasphemous. It is understandable, therefore, that the earliest myths and legends about birdmen usually concern either magicians and men of exceptional gifts, like Daedalus, men of suspect morality, possibly devil-inspired, like Simon Magus, or kings and rulers whose exalted earthly position gave them at least half an excuse to defy the god-ordained nature of things. As speculation about flight descended from legend to reality, so the practice of the half-formed art descended from kings to commoners.

Some of the early aeronauts had a very clear idea of what they would find in the sky once they were airborne. First they would strike a warm region heated by the sun's rays; next a cold layer reaching to the top of the highest mountains in which watery vapours were held; and, finally, a hot upper atmosphere created by the 'fire' of the sun. Once man had struggled through the cold layer—which it was believed played a major part in the formation of rain and snow, clouds, mist, wind and even comets—he entered a place of great serenity, the early philosophers said. But because it was a hot and unstable atmosphere, the man who flew was recommended to stay close to the ground and venture no higher than the cold belt.

As the bird was man's inspiration for flight, early writers held distinct views on its constitution. They believed it contained a high proportion of air and water which gave it the ability to fly. This school of thought was presented by the thirteenth-century German philosopher Bartholomaeus Anglicus, who wrote in his *De Proprietatibus Rerum* that birds were made of a combination of the two most opposite elements—air so they could rise and water to enable them to 'swim' in the atmosphere. As support for this theory, many writers drew on the verse in the Bible from Genesis (Chapter I, verse 20) which said that God had created the birds from water.

Bartholomaeus Anglicus also believed that the bird could 'capture' air in its wings and wrote, "the air contained within the concavity of the feathers lightens the bird and helps to make it rise more easily." It was undoubtedly this philosophy which made many of the early birdmen employ feathers in their 'wings'—or, if not feathers, woven cloth which might similarly 'capture' the air for flight.

The feathers of birds of great power—such as eagles and hawks—were believed to be the best for birdmen's suits, and not a few would-be aeronauts blamed their failure to fly on their having chosen the feathers of the wrong bird. The wings of bats were also seen as adaptable to man's need for flight, and a few of the cloth garments worn by the 'tower jumpers' were modelled on the spans of these nocturnal creatures. (This was not a general practice, however, as the bat was thought by medieval man to be a creature of evil and association with it implied being in league with the Devil.)

For all his study and observation of the bird, however, early man reached several erroneous conclusions about *how* it flew and thereby defeated his objective of flight virtually before he began. He believed, as I have indicated, that the bird 'swam' through the air, moving its wings downwards and backwards, pushing against the air. In fact, as high-speed modern photography has proved, the bird moves its wings downwards and slightly forwards.

Charles H. Gibbs-Smith explains,

The outer four or five of the primary feathers of all birds are differently formed from all their other feathers in that there is little or no vane in front of the shaft, and a large area of vane behind it. The feathers lie, also, nearly at right angles to the body. When the wing beats down, the outer primaries tend to separate, and the air pressure acts on the broad rear vanes and twists each feather into the shape and equivalent of an aeroplane propeller. The rest of the lift necessary to support the bird, as opposed to propelling it forward, is supplied by the secondary feathers of the inner part of the wing.

The up-stroke, or recovery stroke, is made at about twice the speed of the down beat, and provides a certain amount of lift but no thrust forward. The familiar 'whirr' of birds' wings is caused solely by the propelling primaries at the wing tips, which are travelling up and down at a great speed, even in slow-flapping birds.

As modern ornithologists have also noted, birds manœuvre in the air by altering the stretch, camber and angle of their wings, and whenever possible take off and land *into* the wind to get the best possible lift with the least ground speed.

Unaware of his mistakes, man therefore attempted to fly like the bird by beating his home-made wings downwards and backwards in a 'swimming' movement. He also did not comprehend that, although there are some similarities in the bone structure of man and bird, his muscle power—unaided—could never hope to match that of the bird.*

"In a bird," Gibbs-Smith has written on this matter, "the flying muscles may weigh a third or more of the whole bird, thus providing a very powerful engine. In human beings the muscles available for limb movements are far too feeble to be effective. Borelli demonstrated this conclusively in 1680, but would-be birdmen thought they knew better, and have been fruitlessly flapping their artificial wings of cloth, cane, cords, leather thongs and, of course, feathers, ever since."

Fruitless all these endeavours may have been—but what a fascinating story they make: and that is what I have tried to recount in the pages of this book.

In the early chapters we shall discuss the mythology of man-powered flight, going back to the theory that pre-Adamite men could actually fly or levitate—a story supported by a number of authorities—and then move into the realms of recorded time with the legends of Icarus and Wayland the

---

* An interesting comparison between the skeletons of man and bird was made by the aeronautical expert, Professor S. P. Langley, the Secretary of the Smithsonian Institution in America, in an article "The New Flying Machine" published in 1897. Professor Langley is said to have been the man who initiated the serious study of aviation in the United States and lived to see it triumph so spectacularly. I have reproduced the relevant section, complete with illustrations, in Appendix I at the end of this book.

Smith, and the documented accounts of King Bladud and Eilmer of Malmesbury in England, the 'Flying Saracen' of Constantinople and Buoncompagno, the Florentine charlatan.

We shall look at the stories of witches' being able to fly and consider the work of that great genius, Leonardo da Vinci whose theories and designs were to prove the basis and the stimulant for actual flight, generations later. Subsequent chapters will examine the flurry of birdmen who were leaping from towers and buildings throughout Europe for several centuries and how their flights of fantasy became an important theme in literature.

A modern sketch of one of the early 'tower jumpers', clearly showing the ribbed 'wings' with which such men tried to fly

When man at last rises into the atmosphere in a balloon, he appears to be less concerned with attempting to fly under his own power. However, as the aeroplane becomes increasingly sophisticated, the desire for personal achievement and excitement creeps back into his soul, and man-powered flight again occupies his thoughts. With the moon already reached and the planets not far away, it remains one of the last frontiers to be crossed.

To conclude, then, we shall look at the exponents of man-powered flight seeking their ultimate goal under muscle- and pedal-power, the ever-hopeful handful of birdmen, and the fastest growing new solo aeronautical pursuit, hang-gliding.

Our story represents a fascinating element of aeronautical history—an element which its most devoted promoters insist has so often come within a 'wing and a prayer' of success.*

Tiberius Cavallo who wrote an outstanding and perceptive book, *The History and Practice of Aerostation*, in 1785, remarked that the tradition of human flight "might be the result of pure imagination—*or perhaps an art which was lost.*" Before examining the facts as we know them, therefore, it will be interesting to ponder on the question: was all mankind once able to fly?

---

* In December 1975, to test a theory that the Incas of Peru discovered the secret of flight centuries ago, a group of aeronautical experts built a wedge-shaped balloon based on drawings found on Incan ceramics and made of fabric similar to that found in graves by archaeologists. It flew successfully over the plains of Nazco piloted by an Englishman and an American suspended in a basket below.

[2]

Did We All Once Have Wings?

The antiquity of man's desire to fly—it is recorded in text and illustration in the very earliest artefacts—has given rise to a number of fascinating speculations about its origins. While the Ancient Greeks had winged gods, the other ancient civilizations of Egypt, China and the more barbaric European nations also revered beings in the shape of men who possessed the ability to traverse the heavens.

The Christian religion has few more important symbols than the winged angels who were said to provide man's link with God. They must certainly have been the inspiration for many human attempts at flight, being introduced into the imagination of man during his impressionable childhood years. As Charles Gibbs-Smith has written in *A History of Flying*, "In religious households the concept of angels is introduced to children at a very early age; it must therefore be recorded as one of the early influences which have also played their part in the evolution of European aviation. Angels also must have done much to preserve the medieval interest in flying against the counter-influence of those theologians who held that any human attempt to fly was inspired by the Devil."

It has been suggested by some writers that the angels might well have been based on virtual flying men who lived—that is, men who tried to fly with wings and whose abortive efforts were transformed by the passage of time and the distortion of the original oral records into glorious success. It is a thought one can only ponder on and leave to the theologians.

We have seen in the previous chapter that the inspiration for man's wishing to fly might well have been to imitate his gods, or to escape from his natural environment, but the most fascinating theory—though it is impossible to prove—is that man once actually had the ability to fly and then lost it through his own folly. At first sight this might seem a classic case of the crackpot theory; yet its most fervent recent advocate was no less a person than Lord Montague Norman, the first Baron of St Clere and Governor of the Bank of England.

Lord Norman, who died in 1950, is remembered with great affection by colleagues in banking circles, and one of these, Robert Thurston Hopkins, who later became a distinguished scientific and occult investigator, paid this tribute after his death:

> He was a man of mysterious character who had a profound knowledge of hauntings, apparitions, astral travel, levitation and other matters not usually known to London bankers. He dazzled everybody—the intellectual, the dull and the cunning, and even those who worked with him every day. He was like a diamond, gleaming and flashing, full of rainbow variations— now red, now green, now crimson. Yes, just like a diamond—as adamite and bright as that, and his lustre as erratic. It was almost impossible to ever see him the same man twice in a week. You could not locate him. I doubt if he ever located himself; genius nearly always loses itself.

The facts of Lord Norman's life are prosaic in the extreme after such a description, but they underline the character, erudition and learning of the person who propounded such a remarkable theory about the first men. Born in 1871, he was educated at Eton and King's College, Cambridge. He then served in the Bedfordshire Regiment, campaigning in South Africa in 1900–1, where he won the DSO and was mentioned in despatches. After a career as a partner in a London bank, he was made Governor of the Bank of England in 1920 and held this post until 1944, his signature becoming a household word on every sterling bank note. Not a man, obviously, whose opinions deserve anything other than serious consideration.

In his private life, Lord Norman was known to have strong hypnotic powers and a supernatural faculty of perception: his conversation on subjects of this kind could hold an audience of two or three or an entire assembly hall in absolute thrall for as long as he chose.

It was the subject of levitation which apparently first

caused him to speculate on man-flight. He was particularly intrigued by the verses in the Bible (Acts VIII) which read:

39. And when they were come up out of the water, the Spirit of the Lord caught away Philip, that the eunuch saw him no more: and he went on his way rejoicing.
40. But Philip was found at Azotus: and passing through he preached in all the cities, till he came to Caesarea.

Endless theories had, of course, already been advanced about man's ability to levitate or hang suspended in the air, but Lord Norman's unique imagination could not support any traditional ideas. He studied the subject thoroughly and reached the conclusion that man in his cosmic life had possessed all kinds of wonderful facilities in all ages and conditions of space and time, and that one of his normal modes of movement was floating in the air. Gradually, though, as man became pampered and civilized, he adopted what were unnatural habits—such as wearing clothes and breathing incorrectly—and so lost some of the wonderful powers he had once had at his command.

To support his theory, Lord Norman pointed out that flight is a frequent incident in our dreams and he believed this derived from atavistic memory impressions. He expounded this argument in full to Thurston Hopkins, who wrote in his *Ghosts Over England* (1953):

Lord Norman recounted to me how he often had exultant experiences of flying in his dreams, sailing in grand curves and aerial leaps without any great exertion and feeling the thrill of the utterly impossible.
His dreams of flight, he told me, were so real that he felt that the acquisition of this knowledge was something more than a dream; it was a sudden realization of a hitherto unsuspected power. He felt that he had learned to fly just as he had learned to ride a bicycle and that it was an accomplishment he could never forget. Of course, when he awoke he was forced to face the stubborn truth that his dreams had fooled him.
Norman said that for millions of years humanity had probably been making night flights and was curious to discover how this activity, having so little in common with the usual movements of active life, had become a common experience of the life of sleep. He suggested that dream-flights were memory-impressions going back to conditions of life more ancient than

man—life winged and ferocious, with strange animals flying and fighting in the air. Perhaps, he thought, we had, in a slumber, vague memories of things even more ancient than winged prehistoric beasts—the memory of other planets which had perhaps been destroyed in world conflagrations . . . vanished celestial continents with more flexible forces of gravitation, where the normal method of locomotion might have been a kind of gliding, skimming and floating progression.

Hopkins was deeply impressed by Lord Norman's theory, and discussed it with other occult and aeronautical experts—though none shared quite the same enthusiasm. His most interesting exchanges were with another nobleman whose distinguished career of public service and academic qualifications gave especial validity to what he said. This was Air Chief Marshal Lord Dowding, whose profound interest in flight research and air travel led him to make important and far-reaching pronouncements on several controversial aeronautical topics—including flying saucers, which he thought probably existed.

Hugh Dowding was educated at Winchester and served with the RAF during World War I, winning a CMG and a mention in despatches. During the Second World World he was Principal Air ADC to King George VI and was later appointed Air Chief Marshal.

Asked to comment on dream-flight, he told Hopkins,

I think that man of the first and possibly second Root-Race (pre-Adamite) *could* fly or levitate since their bodies contained a high proportion of etheric matter. However, I don't think that that has much to do with flying-dreams. I think they are distorted memories of actual astral travels when the finer bodies leave the physical during sleep.

The implications of this statement immediately created a whole new area of discussion which has already exercised the minds of other experts in various papers and journals. However, the details of this debate are beyond the scope of this book and the reader intrigued by this whole area of thought is advised to seek his own details—firstly about the pre-Adamite peoples and what we know of them, and secondly on levitation and astral travel. It has merely been my intention to present a few details of the fascinating idea that we might all once have flown as naturally as birds. What a thought!

Now, though, we must move beyond speculation and into the realms of fact, and the activities of the first birdmen. Activities, I hasten to add, that have much which is contentious about them—but all of which are inspired by the single desire of man to take wing.

[3]

Birdmen and Tower Jumpers

Any general history of birdmen has, of course, to begin with the classic tale from Greek mythology of Daedalus and his son Icarus and of their winged escape from the island of Crete. But it is as well to bear in mind the remark of Clive Hart:

A woodcut dated 1493 illustrating the legend of Icarus and Daedalus

It seems highly probable that many men of whom nothing is now known flapped feathered arms in vain attempts to rise from the ground, and some may even have met with partial success—just as, in the years preceding and following the successful flights of the Wright brothers, several experimenters managed to build machines which could achieve powered 'hops' of a few yards or more.

E. Charles Vivian in his *History of Aeronautics* (1921) thinks that even the first cavemen may have had the inclination to fly, and argues:

> If the caveman had left records, these would without doubt have shown that he dreamed of flight. His main aim, probably, was self-preservation; when the dinosaur looked around the corner, the prehistoric bird got out of the way in the usual manner—and prehistoric man naturally envied the bird. He may even have tried to improvise these facilities; assuming that he did, there is the ground work of much of the older legend with regard to men who flew, since when history began, legends would be fashioned out of attempts and even the desire to fly, these being compounded of some small ingredient of truth and much exaggeration.

Mr Vivian believes further that it is not beyond the realms of possibility that some cavemen may even have taken to the air by jumping on the backs of the huge birds of the time; though their fate, he agrees, must have been one of great uncertainty!

Ovid provides us with the fullest story of the flight of Daedalus and his beloved son Icarus. Daedalus was a great architect, craftsman and inventor who, having been exiled from Athens, went to the isle of Crete to construct a labyrinth for King Minos to serve as a prison for the fearsome Minotaur, which devoured young maidens. When his task was completed, Daedalus asked for permission to return home, but this was refused by the King.

Thereafter, Ovid tells us, Daedalus vowed to escape: "Minos possesses the earth and the seas; but he does not control the air, and that is the way we shall go if Jupiter pardons the enterprise." The ingenious Greek then devised two sets of wings made of feathers, linen fastenings and wax which he and his son are said to have tried out only briefly before miraculously taking off into the sky. At first the two flew carefully, and at a moderate height, away from the island; they passed Samos, Delos, Maxos and Pros without mishap. Then, says the legend, young Icarus became more daring with his new-found freedom in the air and, despite the warnings of his father, struck out higher. As he rose too close to the sun, the wax of his wings began to melt and the wildly flailing boy crashed down into the sea. The horrified Daedalus could only watch helplessly as his son disappeared beneath the waves, leaving only a few scattered feathers to mark his passing. He flew sadly on to Naples and an embittered old age. The sea where the boy fell is to this day known as the Icarian Sea.

This legend has, as is well known, been an inspiration to artists and writers for generations—of which pictures like that of Peter Breughel (*The Fall of Icarus*) and mentions in books such as James Joyce's *Portrait of the Artist as a Young Man* (the young hero being called Stephen Daedalus) are typical. Also the modern painter and sculptor Michael Ayrton has made a particular study of the story, with its relevance to modern astronauts, and on the personal experience of Icarus —for though his fall proved his mortality, yet he fulfilled the desire to fly.

The story has naturally given rise to much speculation about its actuality. Some commentators believe that it is entirely imaginary, or that it might possibly refer to something quite different from flight—perhaps symbolizing the introduction of sails into navigation, for instance. Patrick Abbot, in his book *Airship* (1973), has suggested that "the myth may have derived from a dimly remembered attempt at 'gliding' by a man of ancient times who expressed one of man's oldest desires."

M. J. B. Davy has probably put the legend in its right perspective when he writes,

> Of all the flying fables of antiquity it seems to have created the most lasting impression on subsequent generations, and it probably stimulated many to imitate. The importance of the story is in its moral effect: Daedalus ('cunning artificer') was a personification of mechanical skill and it was reasonable to suppose that he made some attempts to fly—therein lies the significance of the myth.

On examination of ancient documents, it soon became apparent that these other "flying fables of antiquity" to which Mr Davy refers are widespread throughout the world.

The people of Asia Minor, the Capnobates, for instance, are said to have "travelled by smoke" and this has led to the speculation that they knew the secret of the hot-air balloon. The residents of fabled Atlantis, before it sank beneath the waves, were traditionally supposed to have mastered flight by their own power, as Francis Bacon (1561–1626) wrote in one of his essays. Quoting one of the citizens of the ancient nation, Bacon wrote, "We imitate also the flight of birds; we have some degrees of flying in the air; we have ships and boats for going under water; we have also means to convey sounds in trunks and pipes, in strange lines and distances."

The birdman concept is also to be found in Indian mythology, where legend tells us of Hanouam who fitted himself with wings and sailed through the air, landing in the sacred Lauka. In South America, human flyers are depicted in sculpture and monuments, and some of these statues have formed part of the argument of Erich von Daniken (in his books such as *Chariots of the Gods?*) that men from other worlds visited the earth in spaceships at the dawn of recorded history. Whether the figures are humans with birds' wings, or men from space whose ability to travel in the sky was expressed by the primitive people by giving them the wings of birds, is another matter for conjecture. In any event, there is an important story from the Inca civilization, of the chieftain Ayar Utso, who is said to have made wings and "flown away to the sun".

Egypt has provided us with one of the earliest illustrations of a winged man, in the form of a design on the tomb of the Pharaoh Rameses II which is now kept in the Louvre in Paris. The picture—reproduced elsewhere—shows the great ruler

An ancient Mexican birdman coming to grief—or a man from Space? A puzzling piece of sculpture discussed by Erich von Daniken in *The Gold of the Gods*

of the second millennium BC kneeling on a tower spreading
his artificial wings as if in preparation for flight. Sadly, we do
not know if he made any actual attempts.

The tradition of human flight is also widespread in the
Orient—as Dr Berthold Laufer has reported in his book, *The
Prehistory of Aviation* (1928). Indeed, Dr Laufer believes that
the pursuit in the East actually antedated European endeavour,
but that the latter is better known because of the legends
about it which have become classics. The concept of birdmen is to be found in ancient Chinese mythology, he says,
but he admits that the fables which have been cited as
evidence are often unsatisfactory to the student.

A coherent interpretation of them seems impossible [he
writes]; their essence appears to be pure romance, which is
perhaps understandable when one reflects that it is the marvellous and romantic which lingers in the memory of man. It is
significant that some of the fables have a close parallel in
mythology and legend in the West, but little meaning which is
tangible accrues.

Probably the one Chinese story which has some basis in
fact concerns the Emperor Shun, who lived during the third
millennium BC (approximately 2258–2208). According to details given in the *Annals of the Bamboo Books*, the Emperor
as a young boy, was captured by some enemies of his father,
yet managed to escape by putting on "the work clothes of a
bird" and flying over his prison walls.

This youthful aerial ingenuity seems to have inspired the
Emperor to continue his experiments when he became a man,
and there is a later account in the *Annals* of his jumping
from the top of a tower supported by "two large reed hats"
which must have acted in the same way as a parachute, and
helped him descend to the ground quite safely. Dr Laufer is
inclined to believe this story, as reed hats of the kind mentioned, up to three feet in diameter, are known to have been
made at this time. Of the first story he has his doubts, yet
notes that if it were authenticated it could justifiably be
claimed to be the first attempt in history by a man to fly. (It
is interesting in this context to note that there is a legend that
the Chinese invented the balloon in AD 1300 for the corona-
tion of Empress Fo-King; and that they were the originators
of the kite.)

(*above*) One of the many unknown and intrepid birdmen whose exploits dot the pages of early history — a still from the film *Conquest of the Air*

(*right*) The famous birdman of the classics: the over-adventurous Icarus plunging to earth after flying too close to the sun, while his father Daedalus flies on. . . .

Part of an ancient frieze depicting members of the pre-Adamite race who are said to have had the ability to fly

Illustration from an old Greek vase of the legendary flying creatures, the Sirens, who led unwary sailors to their deaths

Lord Montague Norman, Governor of the Bank of England. He proposed that man was once able to fly, but lost the skill through his own stupidity

Air Chief Marshal Lord Dowding, who also held strong views on the origins of man's desire to fly

The archetypal
Christian angel: was
some long-forgotten
attempt by man to fly
the basis of this
tradition?

"The philosopher
deriding man's attempt
to fly"—a satirical
seventeenth-century
Italian cartoon.

(*above*) Goya's birdmen – the marvellous drawing "Modo de Volar", from his series entitled "Disparates". (*below*) The Valkyrs of Norse legend, who could fly on their aerial steeds or aided by their cloaks of swan feathers

(*top*) An early illustration of a winged man: the Pharaoh Rameses II depicted on his tomb, now in The Louvre. (*below left*) Early seventeenth-century painting by John White of *The Flyer*, an American Indian shaman. (*below right*) An early European birdman, from an illustrated manuscript in the British Museum

The legendary British ruler, King Bladud, who attempted to fly from the Temple of Apollo in London

(*above*) "The Flying Saracen", who made his attempt during festivities in Constantinople in 1162 — from the film *Conquest of the Air*

(*left*) The stained-glass window of Malmesbury Abbey commemorating the "Birdman Monk" Eilmer, who attempted to fly in the eleventh century

In this woodcut dating from 1489 (*right*), the witches have partially changed their shapes in order to ride by broomstick to the Sabbat

(*below*) Modern witches 'flying' around their magic circle at a secret meeting

Witches, accompanied by the Devil, flying off to the Sabbat, and flying around the magic circle with a host of their demons or familiars

(*bottom left*) A witch transforms herself to escape from imprisonment in this fifteenth-century woodcut – but why the mermaid tail? (*below*) An engraving of the Somerset witch Julian Cox; in 1663 she was accused of having flown through the air, and was executed

Leonardo da Vinci, one of the great figures in the history of man's desire to fly, with (*below*) his mechanism for testing an ornithopter wing, and (*bottom*) his remarkable design for a man-powered craft in which the 'pilot' stood upright to work the wings and controls

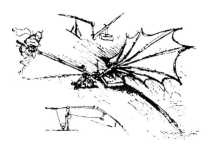

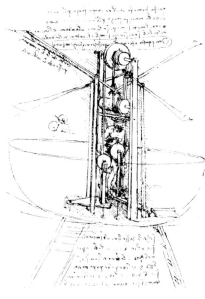

(*above*) The attempted flight of John Damian in Scotland in the early sixteenth century came to a safe if undignified ending in a dunghill (from *Conquest of the Air*). (*below left*) A reconstruction of the attempted flight by Leonardo's contemporary, the Perugian mathematician Giovanni Danti. (*right*) The first illustration of a parachute in history, from Fausto Veranzio's *Machinae Novae* (1595). No viable parachute was made, however, for over two centuries.

The frontispiece of Bishop John Wilkins's important work *Discovery of a New World in the Moone* (1640)

A French illustration of the attempt by the blacksmith Besnier to fly

Man-powered flight was a topic of constant interest in the seventeenth and eighteenth centuries – a typical illustration

A French engraving reflecting the public interest in flight

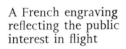

Turkish postage stamp issued 1950 commemorating Hezar-fen Celebi's attempt to fly in the seventeenth century. (*right*) Part of the painting of the flight of the German monk Kaspar Mohr, on the ceiling of the monastery library at Schussenried

A drawing by Gustave Doré for Milton's *Paradise Lost*. The inclined plane may have suggested to Milton the flight of the angel Uriel who travelled between earth and heaven on a ray of sunshine

The remarkable prophet and writer, Daniel Defoe. From a woodcut of 1706

Joseph Addison, who wrote several essays on the folly of man-powered flight

Cyrano de Bergerac's concept of a glass ball which would rise up in the sun's rays

Before closing with China, it should be added that during the Ming period (1368–1644), there seems to have been a widespread belief that flight could be achieved by simply starving oneself to become weightless. It is not recorded how many people tried out this theory—or what number suffered the inevitable result!

I do not believe, however, that there is a more interesting story from antiquity than that of the Norseman Wayland, the blacksmith and maker of precious ornaments, who is said not only to have made wings and flown, but also to have given one of the first lessons in how to manoeuvre a flying machine.

The story of Wayland begins with his encountering three Valkyries—the young and beautiful battle maidens of the god Odin, who occasionally came to earth on horseback and wearing 'swan plumage'. It was said that if a mortal could seize this plumage, he could keep it and the maiden on earth for nine years.

Wayland and two of his brothers happened to see three Valkyries land and remove their plumage for a bathe; so, quietly, they crept up and seized the precious garments and thereby the girls. For nine years, so the story goes, Wayland lived in love and pleasure with his maiden, learning from her the secret of flying with the 'swan plumage'. But at the end of the allotted time she took back her garment and flew off. Wayland, heartbroken, was then an easy prey for one of his old enemies, King Nidud of North Jutland, who knew of his great skill as a smith, and carried him off to imprisonment on one of his islands.

"However, during the pauses in his labour," says H. A. Guerber in *Myths of the Norsemen* (1908), "he fashioned a pair of wings similar to those his wife had used as a Valkyr". Then, with his means of escape ready, Wayland effected revenge on King Nidud by slaying his son.

His act of revenge accomplished [the story goes on], Wayland immediately donned the wings which he had made, and grasping his sword, he rose slowly in the air. Directing his flight to the palace, he perched there out of reach, and proclaimed his crime to Nidud. The King, beside himself with rage, summoned an archer to bring down the impudent bird, but he rose on his wings and flew safely away.

c

In another version of Wayland's story by Didrik of Bern, the smith is said to have escaped from the island by making wings of feathers which had been collected for him by his brother, Egil, who was also a captive. Wayland was apparently unable to do this for himself as he had been incapacitated by the King who had had the tendons of his legs cut to stop him from walking. According to the report, the smith's wings "looked just like the plumage of a bird, flayed off a vulture or the bird called an ostrich".

Didrik describes his eventual escape thus:

Then Wayland asked Egil to put on what he had made and to fly, to see whether it would work. And Egil said, "How shall I go up and fly and come down again?" Then Wayland said, "You must rise against the wind and fly both high and far, but you must come down before the wind." So Egil put on the plumage and flew up into the air as easily as the swiftest bird, but when he came to descend he fell headlong to the earth, striking it so violently that he was almost senseless from the surging in his ears and temples. Then Wayland said, "Tell me, Egil, was this flying costume of any use to you?" And Egil said, "Were it as easy to come down with it as it was to fly, I would now be in another land and you would never have had the flying costume back." And Wayland said, "I will repair what is amiss." Then, with the help of his brother Egil, Wayland himself put on the plumage, swung himself up to the roof of a house, rose into the air and said, "I told you wrong when I told you that you should come down with the wind, because I did not trust you to give me back the flying costume. Know then that all birds come down against the wind and rise in the same way." And with that he flew off and was not seen again.

All in all, I think this is one of the most fascinating and ingenious of all birdmen stories—whether it contains any fact or is wholly fable.

All the stories to this point have, of course, much that is uncertain about them, but we find the first undisputed record of attempted human flight in the exploits of the legendary ninth ruler of Britain, King Bladud.

Much of the life of this man remains shrouded in mystery, although chroniclers declare that he was a skilled necromancer able to work all kinds of magic. (M. J. B. Davy believes that we might interpret this 'neckromanticke art' as the 'scientific' knowledge of the time.) He also earns a footnote in history as the father of King Lear, immortalized by William Shakespeare.

Bladud, who was born in the early years of the ninth century BC, is believed to have studied as a young man at Athens —then the universal centre of learning. On assuming the throne as the ninth king of Britain in 863 BC, he is said to have founded a university at Stamford in Lincolnshire and built the city of Bath where he created the famous hot springs by magical powers. Because of the unsettled nature of his kingdom, Bladud may well have encouraged the population to believe in his necromancy to add weight to his authority.

In any event, he appears to have been convinced that he could fly with the aid of wings, and endeavoured to prove this by leaping from the temple of Apollo in Trinaventum—now the city of London. The only illustration we have of Bladud seems to show that he had more faith in his magical powers keeping him aloft than in his wings, for they are so small that, as one critic has remarked, "not even a cherub could fly upon them".

The old picture of Bladud making his leap is taken from John Taylor's *Memorial of all the English Monarchs*, in which the king's life is described succinctly:

> Bathe was by Bladud to perfection brought,
> By Neckromantick Arts, to flye he sought:
> As from a Towre he thought to scale the Sky,
> He brake his necke, because he soar'd too high.

There are no contemporary descriptions of Bladud's daring leap, and the first brief account is to be found in Geoffrey of Monmouth's *Historia Regum Britanniœ* written about 1147, Fabyn, in his *Chronicle*, compiled in 1516, says of the king:

> This Bladyd taught the lore of Necromancy through his Realme. And fynally toke in it such pryde and presumcion, that he toke upon him to flie into the ayer, but he fell upon the temple of his god Appolyn and thereon was all to torne, when he had ruled Brytayne by the space of XX yeres lauynge after hym a sone named Leyr.

The story of Bladud was reported by several other chroniclers and occurs in the work of some of the Renaissance poets.

Percy Enderbie shared this enthusiasm and recreated the event graphically in his *Works* (1661):

> He poised his body on the twin wings he had made, and hung suspended in the quivering air. Anon, smitten by a longing to gain the sky, he urged his course higher: the nearness of the sun's swift rays softened the perfumed wax that served to bind the wings upon him. An instant, and the wax melted, the arms he moved were now bare of wings: there was nothing to help him and he had no longer any leverage upon the air. And so, destitute of help, he falls headlong, a just reward for his temerity, and breaks his neck.

Aside from the moral tone of the closing sentence, it is interesting to see the close parallels between this account and that of the legend of Icarus. Thoughts which are said to be Bladud's own are repeated in the famous *Mirror for Magistrates*, although as the book is described as "containing the falles of the first unfortunate Princes of this lande", its heavy-handed critique (so typical of many directed against human flight) can hardly be accorded to the king himself:

> Though Magicke Mathematicall,
> Make wooden birdes to flye and sore:
> Eke brasen heads that speake they shall,
> And promise many marveiles more.
>
> I deemde I could more soner frame,
> My selfe to flye then birdes of woode:
> And ment to get eternall fame,
> Which I esteemde the greatest goode.
>
> I deckt my selfe with plumes and winges
> And here thou seest in skilfull wise:
> And many equall poysing thinges,
> To ayde my flight, to fall or rise.
>
> By practise at the length I could,
> Gainst store of winde with ease arise:
> And then which way to light I should,
> And mounte, and turne, I did devise.
>
> Which learned, but not perfectly,
> Before I had there of the sleight:
> I flew aloft but down fell I,
> For want of skill againe to light.

For what should I presume so highe,
Against the cours of nature quite:
To take me winges and saye to flye,
A foole no fowle in fethers dight.

Well then deserts required my fall,
Presumption proude, depruide my breath:
Renowne bereft my life and all,
Desire of praise, procurde my death.

Despite the failure of Bladud's attempt, his inspiration to later generations of birdmen was profound. In Rome, for instance, the idea of man-powered flight exercised the minds of philosophers and rulers for a good many years—though perhaps on a smaller scale than one might have expected of these ingenious people.

The infamous Nero, we are told, believed that he could command men to perform any feat—including that of flight. Dio Chrysostom in his *Discourses* (c AD 110) says of the Emperor:

And no one contradicted him in anything, whatever he said, or affirmed that anything he commanded was impossible to perform. So that even if he ordered anyone to fly, the man promised that too, and for a considerable time he would be maintained in the imperial household in the belief that he would fly.

A specific occasion of 'flight' during Nero's time concerned Simon Magus, the magician—or "the mechanician", as he called himself—who is said to have made experiments at Rome and actually risen in the air. Simon was the founder of an anti-Christian sect with the avowed purpose of proving among other things that there was nothing supernatural about Elijah's flight or the Ascension of Christ. He and his followers claimed that he made several flights using "certain demons" to lift him up. According to Christian teachings, his activities were ended one day in the Forum, where a great crowd had assembled to see him fly. Among the people was the disciple St Peter, who believed that Simon received his power from the Devil, and as the magician rose up into the air, he prayed that God would cancel out this power. Suddenly, Simon let out a cry and crashed down to the ground, breaking his neck. Theologians have rarely disputed that the Roman flew, and attributed his fall to the work of God. However, a modern aeronautical expert, E. Charles Vivian, has wondered if perhaps the "certain demons" which kept Simon aloft were "some primitive form of hot-air balloon or glider" which carried him on the wind? It is an intriguing thought.

Marcus Sabellicus in his *Exemplorum Libri Decem* reports that men could be seen "simulating the flights of birds and rising from the ground" in Rome during the time of Caesar, but later commentators are inclined to the view that these were probably theatrical spectaculars simulated for the sensation-hungry local populace.

Gaius Suetonius also reports that attempts at flight were made during some of the Roman Bacchanalian orgies for the entertainment of the guests. Of one such he writes, "The Icarus at his very first attempt fell close by the imperial couch and bespattered the emperor with his blood". Some prisoners held for the Roman Games were also apparently offered the chance of building wings to fly up from the arena when the wild beasts were released; despite muscle-breaking efforts, all met with bloody ends.

Enforced flights also took place at the famous 'leap' at Leucas, as Strabo writes in his *Geography*:

> It was an ancestral custom among the Leucadians, every year at the sacrifice performed in honour of Apollo, for some criminal to be flung from this rocky look-out for the sake of averting evil, wings and birds of all kinds being fastened to him, since by their fluttering they could lighten the leap, and also for a number of men, stationed all round below the rock in small fishing boats, to take the victim in, and, when he had been taken on board, to do all in their power to get him safely outside their borders.

Only one Greek inventor seems to have pursued the lead given by his countryman Daedalus, a man named Archytas of Tarntum (428–347 BC) the friend of Plato, who launched into the air a "flying stag". According to chronicles, he also made a "pigeon of wood" which apparently flew "but which could not raise itself again after having fallen". It's flight was said to have been accomplished by a "mechanical contrivance" and some modern commentators believe the pigeon probably hung from a whirling arm and was driven by a jet of steam. Clive Hart, on the other hand, believes "it is more likely to have been a glider or an attempt at the rocket bird".

Corinthian

Restaurant & Lounge Bar

Lunches, Dinners, Pre-Show Meals, Weddings and Celebrations.
Tel: 01438 242623/242610 for further details.

Arts & Leisure Centre, Lytton Way,
Stevenage SG1 1LZ
Conference Office: 01438 242648
Catering Office: 01438 242623
Restaurant: 01438 242610
Fax: 01438 242675

Grant-aided by

SteVenage BOROUGH COUNCIL

CORINTHIAN RESTAURANT

RESTAURANT PROMOTION

PRE THEATRE SUPPER
£9.50 (three courses)
To reserve your table please telephone

Stevenage Leisure Limited

Apart from the Greeks and the Romans, the Arabs too were experimenting with flight, as two examples show. In AD 852, the Arab savant Armen Firman is said to have attempted flight at Córdoba. He jumped from a tower with a canvas cloak fixed to his body, and though he fell rapidly earthward "there was enough air within the folds of his cloak to prevent great injury when he reached the ground".

Just over twenty years later, a physician named Abbas b. Firnas had a spectacular success, if we are to believe contemporary reports. The attempt took place in Andalusia about 875 and is reported by the historian al-Makkari in *The History of the Mohammedan Dynasties in Spain*:

> Among other very curious experiments which he made, one is his trying to fly. He covered himself with feathers for the purpose, attached a couple of wings to his body, and, getting on an eminence, flung himself into the air, when, according to the testimony of several trustworthy writers who witnessed the performance, he flew to a considerable distance, as if he had been a bird, but in alighting again on the place where he had started, his back was very much hurt, for not knowing that birds when they alight come down upon their tails, he forgot to provide himself with one.

Although modern commentators believe Firnas may have glided for some distance, his return to the place from which he started was certainly a piece of dramatic licence. The mention of a tail makes the story particularly interesting, as the inventor obviously appreciated its importance in flight and was certainly among the very first to do so.

Another dubious man-flight is reported from Persia between AD 241 and 272 and noted by Berthold Laufer in *The Prehistory of Aviation*. The story concerns an architect who built a tower in Hamadhan for King Shapur I. Laufer writes:

> The jealous king decided to leave the master builder on the top of the tower, as he did not want anyone else to profit by his genius. The architect consented, but asked one favour of the king: that he be permitted to erect a wooden hut on the tower to protect his body from the attack of vultures. The king granted the request and ordered that he was supplied with as much timber as he needed. Then the architect was abandoned to his fate. He took up his tools, made a pair of wings from the wood left with him, and fastened them to his body. Driven

by the wind he rose into the air and landed unscathed at a safe place, where he kept in hiding.

Among all the tales of success in these early times, historians have found only one instance where complete failure is reported: that of the Turkestan lexicographer, Abu al-Djawhari, who spent his life travelling and gathering material for his studies, mainly among the desert people. Whether his constant exposure to the blinding sun affected his reason is not known, but some time about AD 1002 he stood on the roof of a mosque in Nisabur where he was teaching and announced that he would amaze the world by performing a feat never before accomplished. He then showed that he had strapped two large wooden wings to his body and jumped into the air. He plunged straight to the ground and was killed instantly.

Once into the Middle Ages, we find a changing attitude towards human flight, as M. J. B. Davy has noted:

> The element of superstition is absent and it is replaced by what is clearly a human motive—the ambition to perform a feat wonderful and unique. The idea of flight, expressed in mythology as a supernatural attribute, became rational with the realization that it was a physical phenomenon.

One of the first men to approach flight in this way was a learned Benedictine monk in the Abbey at Malmesbury, known as Eilmer. (His name is sometimes incorrectly given as Oliver.) Eilmer may well have been aware of the earlier attempts at flight—particularly those of his near-contemporary Abu al-Djawhari. (Several authorities credit the Arabs in general with being responsible for the infiltration into medieval Europe of Oriental ideas about flying.) In any event his feat, sometime between AD 1020–1040 and now seen as the first substantial glide in the history of flight, is recorded by the authoritative William of Malmesbury in his *Chronicle*:

> He was a man learned for those times, of ripe old age, and in his early youth had hazarded a deed of remarkable boldness. He had by some means, I scarcely know what, fastened wings to his hands and feet so that, mistaking fable for truth, he might fly like Daedalus, and collecting the breeze on the summit of a tower he flew for the distance of a furlong. But agitated by the violence of the wind and the swirling of the air,

as well as by awareness of his rashness, he fell, broke his legs, and was lame ever after. He himself used to say that the cause of his failure was his forgetting to put a tail on the back part.

Milton, in his *History of Britain* (1670), also stresses this lack of a tail bringing the endeavour to a sorry conclusion. He writes:

> Eilmer in his youth strangely aspiring, had made and fitted Wings to his Hands and Feet; with these on the top of a Tower, spread out to gather air, he flew more than a Furlong; but the wind being too high, came fluttering down, to the maiming of all his limbs; yet so conceited of his Art, that he attributed the cause of his fall to the want of a Tail, as Birds have, which he forgot to make to his hinder parts.

Although there may have been a considerable element of luck in Eilmer's actual flight of "120 paces", because of the contemporary reports which exist, the claim that he was "the first man to have flown in Europe" seems fully justified. (His adventure is marked today in Malmesbury by a stained-glass window in an alcove in the Abbey, and by a public house, "The Flying Monk" in the town itself.)

Crippling injuries were to be the only reward a Turkish birdman achieved when he took off from the top of the tower of the hippodrome in Constantinople in 1162. The man attempted his flight during festivities being held for Kilij Arslan, the Sultan of Rum, during his visit to Manuel Comnenus, the Greek Emperor, who had successfully campaigned on his behalf. The event is described by the English historian Richard Knolles in his *Genrall Historie of the Turks* (1603):

> Amongst the quaint devices of many for solemnizing so great a triumph, there was an active Turk, who had openly given it out, that against an appointed time, he would, from the top of a high tower in the tilt yard, fly the space of a furlong; the report whereof had filled the city with a wonderful expectation of so great a novelty. The time prefixed being come, and the people without number assembled, the Turk, according to his promise, upon the top of a high tower shewed himself, girt in a long large white garment, gathered into many plaits and foldings, made on purpose for the gathering of the wind; wherewith the foolish man had vainly persuaded himself to have

hovered in the air, as do birds upon the wings, or to have guided
himself, as are ships with their sails. Standing thus hovering a
great while, as ready to take his flight, the beholders still laugh-
ing and crying out, "Fly, Turk, fly! How long shall we expect
thy flight?", the Emperor in the meantime still kept dissuading
him from so desperate an attempt; and the sultan, betwixt fear
and hope, hanging in doubtful suspense what might happen to
his countryman. The Turk after he had a great while hovered
with his arms abroad (the better to have gathered the wind, as
birds do with their wings), and long deluded the expectation of
the beholders, at length finding the wind fit, as he thought,
for this purpose, committed himself with his vain hope into the
air; but instead of mounting aloft, this foolish Icarus came
tumbling down with such violence, that he broke his neck, his
arms, his legs, with almost all the bones of his body.

The Saracen's flying garment—a sort of parachute glider—
was apparently made of linen and braced with rods of willow-
wood on a framework. Unfortunately, as another report puts
it, "the weight of his body having more power to drag him
down than the wings to sustain him, he broke his bones and
his evil plight was such that he did not long survive".

Despite his failure, this anonymous Turk has a special place
in our history as one of the earliest authenticated 'tower
jumpers'—the men who from time to time have jumped off
high buildings equipped with artificial wings or billowing
cloaks.

The Saracen certainly had more courage and nerve than
an Italian named Buoncompagno who announced in 1232 that
he would fly—and then backed down at the last moment.
(He was probably not the only would-be birdman to have a
change of heart at the last moment, but his remains the sole
early incident which is on record.)

Buoncompagno, who came from Florence and can best be
described by the modern term as being a confidence trickster,
sought to exploit the population of Bologna with his claim.
On the day on which he had said he would fly—reports Salim-
bene de Adam in the *Cronica* (c 1287) the whole population
gathered at the foot of a hill just outside the city. Buoncompagno, fitted with wings on his arms, stared down at the
assembly of men, women and children for some time and then
announced, "Depart with divine Benediction, and let it suffice

that you have looked upon the face of Buoncompagno." The people did indeed depart—driving the hapless man before them with stones and cries of derision!

At this time, another Italian, one Giovanni da Fontana, was similarly intrigued by the public interest in flight and had ideas as to how it might be promoted—but with rather more honourable intentions than Buoncompagno.

Fontana's main interest was in the concept of 'rocket birds' and how they might be made to fly, as he propounded in his classic work, *Metrologum de Pisce Cane et Volucre*. However, in the course of his study, he had given thought to the problems of man-powered flight and written:

> I, indeed, have no doubt that it is possible to attach to a man wings which may be artificially moved, by means of which he will be able to raise himself into the air and move from place to place and climb towers and cross water, on which subject I some time ago began to write and set forth my ideas, but being distracted by other activities I never completed the work. Many others have risen by means of cords and ladders and such like apparatus. But the discussion of these things I shall put aside until I have a better opportunity at another time.

Sadly, Fontana's "better opportunity at another time" never arose and his technical mind was not brought to bear on the problem. However, another man in Europe was already deliberating on the whole issue of flight—the man who, in effect, inaugurated the era of scientific speculation on the topic: Roger Bacon.

Experts are, of course, divided in their opinions about Bacon's contribution to aeronautics, and some of his 'discoveries', once applauded, are now treated with amusement. Yet Bacon did clearly outline a kind of flying machine and is the first writer to treat the subject rationally. As M. J. B. Davy has said:

> He represents a landmark in human development, and though actually he contributed nothing to the subject of flight, his reference to it being merely a passing comment, the spirit which prompted that and his many other observations was remarkable in so far as it marked a stage in the escape of the human mind from its original limitations. With regard to the age-long problem of flight, his standpoint was that ideas should be tested by experiment and that none, unless so proved, should

be accepted. The method was that now known as 'scientific'; it made use of logic, but it viewed the finding with distrust until verified by experiment.

Bacon, who lived from 1214 to 1292, studied at Oxford and Paris and became a Franciscan monk. Backing up his theory about scientific study, he experimented in many fields and in his writing predicted amongst other things steam locomotives, the hydrostatic press and even gave the first coded formula in Europe for the making of gunpowder.

His reference to flight was made in *De Mirabili Potestate Artis et Naturae* (1250) which, in its first English translation, read:

> Yea, instruments to flie withall, so that one sitting in the middle of the Instrument, and turning about an Engine, by which the wings being artificially composed may beate the ayre after the manner of a flying bird. . . . And it is certaine that there is an instrument to flie with, which I never saw, nor know any man that hath seen it, but I full well know by name the learned man that invented the same.

Bacon discusses the concept no more fully than this, although he does sketch a flying machine in the same treatise. In hindsight, it may well be his last remark about knowing a learned man who had invented a flying machine which led to the numerous highly coloured and totally false accounts that he himself flew.

Despite Bacon's attitude to flight, and the earlier experiments of the birdmen and tower jumpers, the search for the secret of flight fell away dramatically thereafter. There was a little speculation on the part of Albertus Magnus, Albert of Saxony, and one or two other thirteenth- and fourteenth-century philosophers, but in essence their work did no more than keep a flickering flame of interest alight. As Charles Gibbs-Smith has written,

> Both speculation, experiment and tower jumping then subsided for about two centuries—probably influenced by the taint of sorcery on such ideas—except for the practice of broomstick aviation by witches.

It is the remarkable claim that witches and those who belonged to their dark league could actually fly that we shall examine next before moving on to the birth of aeronautics in the fifteenth century at the hands of Leonardo da Vinci. And in studying the alleged aerial powers of the witches, we shall at last explain after centuries of mystery and controversy what they *actually* did. . . .

[4]

The Flying Witches – A Myth Exploded

There is contained in a remarkable seventeenth-century Swedish manuscript about witchcraft the following 'confession' by a group of witches from the villages of Mohra and Elfdale about how the Devil enabled them to fly:

> Then he [the Devil] asked us whether we would serve him with soul and body. If we were content to do so, he set us upon a beast which he had there ready, and carried us over churches and high walls; and after all we came to a green meadow where Blockula lies. We must procure some scrapings from altars, and filings of church clocks; and then he gives us a horn with salve in it, wherewith we do anoint ourselves (chrism); and a saddle with a hammer (Thor's); and a wooden nail, thereby to fix the saddle (Walkyr's); whereupon we call upon the Devil and away we go.
>
> For the journey, we made use of all sorts of instruments, of beasts, of men, of spits and posts, according as we had opportunity; if we do ride upon goats (Azazel) and have many children with us, that all may have room, we stick a spit into the backside of the goat, and then are anointed with the aforesaid ointment. What the manner of our journey is, God only knows.

Although this statement is of a comparatively late date in the history of witchcraft—the first persons were being denounced and punished for the practice in the thirteenth century—it is typical of many others from all over Europe dealing with the allegation that witches could fly. This attribute was universally accorded to them, and they were said to achieve it either by direct contact with the Devil—who used his own special brand of magic to perform the act—or by riding on a broomstick, or by rubbing on themselves a 'flying ointment' of the kind described by the Swedish villagers.

The very earliest record of flying by supernatural means seems to date from the ninth century, and though scholars evidently denounced it as an "illusion of devils", the belief persisted.* A century later it was thought to be a skill possessed only by "wicked women" as the *Canon Episcopi* claimed, noting that they "ride upon certain beasts with the pagan goddess Diana, and fly over vast tracts of country."

The Druids were also said to be in possession of this secret, and in the twelfth-century manuscript the *Coir Anmann* there is the account of a Druid named Fullon who was the first in his order to "cast a spell on a wisp so as to send thereby a human being flying."

It was with the widespread persecution of suspected witches by the various Christian religious orders of Europe that witchcraft and flying really became inextricably linked. The assumption is not difficult to understand when one learns that the eminent theologians of the time believed implicitly that since Christ had been carried to the top of a mountain by Satan, there was no reason why the Evil One should not similarly transport his own disciples—either on the backs of spirits under his command or through other more human agencies.

The populer idea is, of course, of the witch's flying on a broomstick, but a thorough examination of the multitude of documents shows that there are in fact remarkably few such incidents specifically recorded. (The broom, originally made of a stalk of the broom plant with a bunch of leaves bound on the head, traditionally symbolized domesticity and womanhood.)

* There is an earlier story from the eighth century, which, though not often repeated today, may well have influenced attitudes about witchcraft and flight. It is recorded in John Goldstrom's *Narrative History of Aviation* (1930): "There still persists a Swiss legend that about AD 790 some now-forgotten experimenters living near Mount Pilatus in Switzerland forced several poor wretches of the community to ascend in a balloon-like contivance. They were said to have descended in the town of Lyons, and there were mobbed as sorcerers. They were condemned to be burned to death. But Bishop Agobard elected to question them, after which he decided that they were harmless liars, and they were released. Afterwards Bishop Agobard wrote a book on the superstitions of the time, and logically proved the impossibility of human flight. Belief in the ability of sorcerers to fly, and witches to travel on broomsticks through the air, persisted, however, for many centuries."

Perhaps the earliest reference to a witch riding a broomstick is the historian Holinshed's story of the fourteenth-century Irish witch, Alice Kyteler. She had a broom on which "she ambled and galloped through thick and thin, when and in what manner she listed after having greased it with the ointment which was found in her possession."

The *Errores Gazariorum* published in 1450 maintained that a stick with flying ointment was presented to every witch after she had shown her allegiance to the Devil at her initiation by kissing him on the rectum (the notorious 'kiss of shame'). This view was supported to a degree by the theologian Lambert Daneau in his *Les Sorciers* (1564); he believed that the Devil aided those witches "that are so weak that they cannot travel of themselves" and to them he "gave a rod and certain ointment".

One of the rare records of a witch actually confessing to having flown on a broomstick occurred in 1453 when a certain Guillaume Edelin stated that she had done so at St Germain-en-Laye near Paris. A witch of Savoy, tried in 1477, also said that the Devil gave her a long stick and jar of ointment and she merely had to rub the liquid on the rod, place it between her legs, and call out, "Go, in the Devil's name, go!" and she would be transported through the air to the witches 'Sabbat' or meeting.

Several other phrases are recorded as having been used by the witches to aid their flight. In her confession, the Scottish witch, Isobel Gowdie (May 1662) said that, "When we wold ryd, we tak windlestrawes or bean stakes, and put them betwixt owr foot, and say thryse, 'Horse and hattock, horse and goe; Horse and pellatis, ho! ho!' And immediatlie we flie away whair evir we wold."

Lady Jane Wilde, the mother of Oscar Wilde, reports in her study of Irish superstition, *Ancient Legends, Mystic Charms and Superstitions of Ireland*, that witches in her country would put on a red cap when they wished to go to the Sabbat and cry, "By yarrow and rue, and my red cap too, hie over to England."

According to Martin Tuloff, French witches straddled a broomstick and were whisked up the chimney by shouting, "Go in the name of the Devil and Lucifer over rocks and thorns". Though witches were traditionally always supposed to leave their homes by way of the chimney, this is one of the very few instances where it is actually recorded.

The American witches in New England were also supposed to have a secret formula for flying, but with the single exception of the case of Ann Foster who, in 1692, was alleged to have flown to a witch-meeting on a pole, there are no other reports of the activity.

The most fully documented case we have of a witch flying refers to an aged Somersetshire woman, Julian Cox, who was tried before the Somerset Summer Sessions in August 1663. This unfortunate soul was indicted for bewitching an unnamed serving girl, and the main evidence against her was that a witness had seen her "fly into her own chamber window in her full proportion". In reply to these charges, the 70-year-old woman said that though she had been tempted into witchcraft by three persons who "came riding towards her upon three broomstaves, borne up about a yard and a half from the ground", she steadfastly resisted their blandishments. She protested that she had never committed any witchcraft, but was still found guilty by the judge and executed.

Later commentators have seen these eye-witness stories of 'broomstick rides' for what they undoubtedly were, superstitious fear, hallucination or tricks of the evening light. (If the witches did 'ride' their broomsticks at all, it was probably at their secret assemblies where they stuck them between their legs as they danced in a circle performing a fertility rite: but even this is highly contentious.)

The explanation as to what happened when the witches rubbed themselves with 'flying ointment', though, is not quite so easily explained.

The history of witchcraft is well served with accounts of the ointments which the witches were supposed to have rubbed on their bodies to enable them to fly. Reginald Scot, the author of that famous study, *Discoverie of Witchcraft* (1584) gives two recipes for these potions in his book:

I. The fat of yoong children, and seeth it with water in a brasen vessell, reserving the thickest of that which remaineth boiled in the bottome, which they laye up and keep, untill occasions serveth to use it. They put hereunto *Eleoselinum*, *Aconitum*, *Frondes populeas*, and *Soote*.

II. *Sium, acarum vulgarem, pentaphyllon*, the blood of a flitter

D

mouse, *solanum somniferum* and *oleum*. They stampe all these together, and then they rubbe all parts of their bodies exceedinglie, til they looke red, and be verie hot, so as the pores may be opened, and their flesh soluble and loose. They joine herewithall either fat, or oil in stead thereof, that the force of the ointment maie the rather pearse inwardly, and so be more effectuall. By this means in a moonlight night they seeme to be carried in the aire.

A number of other sixteenth- and seventeenth-century writers also give details of the ingredients, which invariably contained extracts from strongly poisonous plants. Among those most commonly listed were deadly nightshade, henbane, aconite and hemlock. Other constituents included cinquefoil, sweet flag, poplar leaves, parsley, soot and some kinds of oil.

Scot, in common with other writers, mentions certain revolting additions to these potions, such as the corpses of children who had been stolen from their homes or dug up from their graves. These bodies were supposedly "seethed in a cauldron" and the resultant grease was used as the basis for the flying ointment; the bowels and other intestines were sometimes said to be thrown in for good measure.

In hindsight, these additions were probably pure invention on the part of the persecutors of witchcraft to make the crimes of the suspects seem more horrendous. They would certainly have had no special effects, and indeed normal household oil would serve better as an unguent. (Other authorities have suggested that practitioners themselves claimed that such ingredients were incorporated to protect the secret of their formulæ and inspire awe and a little fear in those who consulted them.)

An early account of the use of 'flying ointment' is revealed in the testimony of five women accused of witchcraft in northern France in 1460. They said that the Devil had given them a salve which they rubbed on their hands and on a small wooden rod, and with this between their legs they "flew above good towns and woods and waters to their meeting place".

A notable occasion is recorded in England in 1664, when a group of Somerset witches said that before they went to their meetings they smeared their wrists and forearms with a greenish oil which 'smells raw'. To help this portion whisk them away to their Sabbats, the women said, they also uttered the words, "Thout, tout a tout, tout, throughout and about".

Though for centuries most of the population of both high and low rank believed that the witches could fly with this magic ointment, the truth was already beginning to emerge as early as 1560. In his *Magiae Naturalius*, Johannes Porta related how a witch had promised to demonstrate her powers to him by obtaining in a few hours information from a town several days' journey away. The woman then shut herself in a room, and, unaware that Porta was watching her through a crack,

Ointments containing hallucinogenic drugs were rubbed on the body to produce 'visions' of flight: an illustration from Guazzo's *Compendium Maleficarum*

undressed and rubbed ointment all over herself. She immediately appeared to go into a trance, the author reports, so he went into the room and tried to rouse her. Though he shook her severely and even beat her until her skin was bruised, she did not awaken. Later, when she did come round, "she said she had travelled over seas and mountains and other impossibilities". Though Porta insisted that she had never left the room and showed the bruises he had himself inflicted to prove the point, "she still steadfastly declared that she had flown".

Fifty years later, Francis Bacon went further with these suspicions in his *Sylva Sylvarum* (1680):

The ointment that witches use is reported to be made of the fat of children digged out of their graves; of the juices of smallage [wild celery], wolfbane and cinquefoil, mingled with the meal of fine wheat, but I suppose that the soporiferous medicines are likest to do it.

Bacon, though he received little support, had hit the nail squarely on the head. His opposition, though, was formidable; the Church had no doubts on the matter, as Francesco Guazzo stated in his immensely influential though harshly bigoted *Compendium Maleficarum* (1626), "Those who assert that it is not true, but only a dream or an illusion, certainly sin in lack of true reverence to our mother the church".

Even with the later dawning of rationality where witchcraft was concerned, the theologians still could not dismiss the connection between witches and flying from their minds, as Professor Russell Hope Robbins notes in his *Encyclopaedia of Witchcraft and Demonology* (1959):

They arrived at several solutions, but generally found the simplest way to prove guilt was to equate the delusion with the act. Consequently, a woman who in her own mind (even if dreaming) considered she had flown to the Sabbat was just as guilty as if she had physically mounted a real broom and been physically carried aloft.

Today, scientific study of the constituents of these ointments has proved beyond all reasonable doubt that they contained strong stimulants which would induce all manner of 'flights of fancy' in the mind of the person on whose body they were rubbed. Professor A. J. Clarke, for one, has pointed out in an appendix in the *Witch Cult in Western Europe* that the strong poisons contained in flying ointments would have definite psychological effects, especially if rubbed into skins broken by scratches or the bites of vermin.

For instance, deadly nightshade is a powerful poison acting locally on the sensory nerve-endings and also on the central nervous system. Therefore a large dose would induce "general excitement, restlessness, vertigo, talkativeness, laughter and disturbance of vision, giving rise to illusions generally of a pleasing character", according to pharmacologist Walter E. Dixson. The well-known effect of dilation of the pupils of the eyes, he adds, might well assist in the production of the illusion of sight—the seeing of visions. Similarly, henbane contains potent alkaloids which produce illusions, while aconite acts on the heart and breathing, producing tingling, numbness and anaesthesia. Hemlock tends to produce loss of muscular power and eventual paralysis.

The effects of these poisons, liberally mixed with the other less harmful ingredients, can therefore clearly be seen as having stimulated the highly susceptible minds of men and women during the witchcraft 'era' into believing they 'flew' to satanic orgies when in fact they never even left their homes. So, almost sadly, after centuries of grandilouquent debate the secret of flight that the practitioners of witchcraft possessed can be explained in terms of simple drug-induced delusions.

Modern followers of witchcraft—now practised as an ancient pre-Christian fertility cult—do, however, still retain a reminder of this ability which is credited to them in their initiation ceremonies. As witchcraft expert Cecil Williamson explained recently, "Nowadays their flights usually take place as an initiation ordeal. What happens is that they are given a drugged drink, then told to take a running jump with a long pole and launch themselves across some local 'Devil's Leap'. Subsequently, they are caught in a net. Afterwards they remember having flown. And who is to say they didn't?"

But enough of witch flights, such illusions must now give way in our history to reality as we return to the history of man-powered flight to discuss the scholar who effectively gave birth to the art of aeronautics, the great Leonardo da Vinci.

[5]

Leonardo and the Birth of Aeronautics

Perched on a hillside over the beautiful renaissance city of Florence stands the picturesque little town of Fiesole. The road up to it from the city is not easy to find, and visitors who do not speak Italian and seek directions from passers-by are most likely to be answered with "Fiesole? Fiesole is up", and a finger pointed dramatically towards the sky. There is, in fact, something rather appropriate about these directions, for it was from Fiesole 'up in the sky', so the story goes, that Leonardo da Vinci made several unsuccessful attempts to fly in the fifteenth century.

The story of this great man is, of course, filled with tales of conjecture and speculation; but what is beyond dispute is that he was the first man to record some rational principles of flight. As M. J. B. Davy has said in *Air Power and Civilization* (1941):

> The age of true scientific speculation on the subject may be said to have begun with his coming, though the results of his investigations were not made known to the world until 1797 when his manuscripts were first discussed, having been brought by Napoleon from Italy to Paris in the previous year. The research of Leonardo could have therefore—as in the case of Roger Bacon—no influence whatever on other investigators for some three centuries, though it is possible that his work in regard to flight was known to a few of his contemporaries.

Aside from his achievements in the realms of aeronautical designs—which we shall examine later—one of the most fascinating and still unanswered questions about Leonardo is whether, as part of his research, he himself flew. Just under a hundred years ago, balloonist Henry Coxwell put a long-held rumour into print when he wrote in his *Wonderful Balloon Ascents* (1887) "Leonardo da Vinci might have known the art of flying in the air, and might even have practised it. A statement to this effect, at least, is found in several histories. We have, however, no direct proof of the fact."

Indeed, one has to agree with Coxwell that one has no direct evidence that the master flew; but the circumstantial evidence is very strong and I believe a case can be made that Leonardo was not only an aeronautical genius, but a determined birdman, too.

There is little doubt that, in the main, Leonardo was more

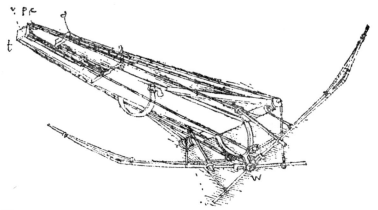

The complete design for Leonardo's man-powered craft in which it was said he actually flew

interested in the formation of workable ideas that in actually putting them into practice. However, if we accept the words of several experts, he became 'obsessed' with the idea of man-powered flight and drove himself harder towards its accomplishment than virtually any of his other objectives. He certainly built models of his flying machines and there seems every likelihood that he also constructed full-scale versions of one or more of them for actual trials.

In Florence, and Fiesole in particular, people will insist that Leonardo flew, quoting traditions handed down for centuries and therefore not the most conclusive of evidence. These stories apparently arose less than a generation after the great man's death, and some modern residents even claim to be able to point out the hillside from which he launched himself into the air. The most scholarly direct the enquirer to two authorities who wrote on the matter shortly after Leonardo's death.

G. Cardano, a virtual contemporary of Leonardo, discusses flight briefly in his *De Subtilitate* (1550) and says that he "tried, but in vain". The Frenchman P. Boaistuau, writing his *Bref Discours de l'Excellence et Dignité de l'Homme* in 1558, sees the conquest of the air being close at hand, especially as Leonardo "has so nearly achieved that aim". Cuperus, who wrote a *Treatise on the Excellence of Man*, actually asserts "on good authority" that the great Italian did fly.

However, if we carefully search Leonardo's own voluminous writings, the most important evidence seems to lie there. In several of the manuscripts—along with the sketches of flying machines—are passages which describe how these might be made with cane, reed, linen, taffeta, fustian, paper, greased leather thongs and, where appropriate, springs made of wire. In a specific entry for 1st January 1496, he describes preparing the glue for binding the materials and adds that "Tomorrow morning on the second day of January, I will make the thong and the attempt".

On another manuscript page he says more directly still, "From the mountain which takes its name from the great bird [Monte Ceceri—Swan Mountain—near Fiesole], the famous bird will take its flight, which will fill the world with great renown".

No understatement this: for if Leonardo had flown and left more direct evidence, his genius would take on a still greater dimension.

If we look carefully at his papers, we also find that the engineer has given instructions that tests are best carried out over water—viz: "This machine should be tried over a lake, and you should carry a long wine-skin as a girdle so that in case you fall you will not be drowned." The voice of experience, perhaps?

Students have similarly discovered that he left notes about suspending a version of one of his machines from the roof of the cathedral in Milan. He would then climb up into the machine, he said, and see if by working the wings he could make it rise enough to slacken the tension on the rope. Charles Gibbs-Smith has written of this in *Leonardo da Vinci's Aeronatics* (1967), "It is just possible, but highly unlikely, that Leonardo built one of his machines and lay in it fruitlessly flapping its wings; its weight alone would have kept it firmly earthbound".

Another authority who has been fascinated by these stories is Clive Hart, and he has concluded in *The Dream of Flight*: "While passages in his work suggest that cautious attempts of some kind were made, Leonardo never followed them up with any notes on the results of his experiments. This may well have been due to a reluctance to commit to paper any record of failure."

Whether or not Leonardo **tried** to fly and failed—and I find myself very much inclined **to** the view that he did—we

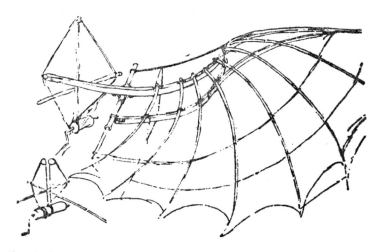

Sketch by Leonardo of his design for a bird-shaped wing to be operated by a hand winch

can be sure about what he did achieve in the way of designing man-powered aircraft by looking at his drawings and sketches which remain with us to this day. During his lifetime, 1452–1519, he seems to have often absorbed himself in the matter, as the 160 pages of manuscript which comprise the work *Sul Volo Degli Uccelli* (*On the Flight of Birds*)—completed in Florence in 1505—show.

From quite early on in his life, the fundamental idea which he pursued was that human flight could be achieved by imitating nature mechanically through close study of bird flight. This he evidently did with considerable energy, and later he wrote:

A bird is an instrument working according to mathematical law, which instrument it is within the capacity of man to reproduce with all its movements, but not with a corresponding degree of strength, though it is deficient only in the power of maintaining equilibrium. We may therefore say that such an instrument constructed by man is lacking in nothing except the life of the bird, and this life must needs be supplied from that of man.

The life which resides in the bird's members will, without doubt, better conform to their needs than will that of man which is separated from them, and especially in the almost imperceptible movements which preserve equilibrium. But since we see that the bird is equipped for many obvious varieties of movements, we are able from this experience to deduce that the most rudimentary of these movements will be capable of being comprehended by man's understanding; and that he will to a great extent be able to provide against the destruction of that instrument of which he has himself become the living principle and the propeller.

With these principles in mind, he began to evolve a series of machines with flapping wings—his 'ornithopters'. He realized that man's arms alone were not strong enough to work the wings, so he designed a mechanism which also brought the legs into play. "Write of swimming in the water," he said, "and you will have the flight of the bird through the air."

What he did not fully appreciate, however, was the manner in which a bird flies (as I have explained in Chapter 1), and that man's total muscular power would never be enough to achieve what he had in mind. He did, though, clearly understand gliding and soaring flight, and—as Charles Gibbs-Smith has pointed out—he had a brilliant flash of insight about streamlining. "If only he had concentrated his attention on this sphere," the historian writes, "he might have constructed and flown a full-sized rigid-wing glider and anticipated Lilienthal by four centuries."

Some biographers have asserted that Leonardo—in all his

other experimentation so objective—became obsessed with his search for human flight and in doing so refused to allow himself to see the basic flaws in his arguments. Certainly, he is known to have frequently expressed a desire for the power and freedom of birds and often went into the Florentine markets to buy caged birds from the traders and set them free. Wings also dominate his art, and his "Angel of the Annunciation" seems a natural as well as a supernatural flyer. Leo Valentin, himself a searcher after man-powered flight as well as a biographer of the great Italian, has said that his concern for flying was "the most tremendous, most obsessing, most tyrannical of his dreams".

In pursuit of his dream, Leonardo designed several kinds of man-powered ornithopters, an ornithopter powered by a

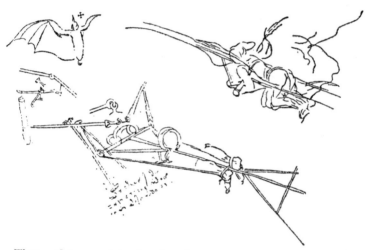

Three of Leonardo's sketches for a man-powered ornithopter

spring motor, a partial glider with flapping wing tips, a number of machines which are best classified as 'flying chariots', and some apparatus for directional control and wind testing.

In the context of this book, it is in the two basically different types of man-powered ornithopters that we are most interested. The first is the 'prone' type in which the operator lies in a wooden frame and moves either two or four wings by means of the system of levers and foot stirrups (See p. 55)

The second is the 'standing' ornithopter where the operator stands upright and works a somewhat more complicated mechanism which again activates the two or four artificial wings. (See illustration.) Accompanying his sketches for these craft, Leonardo stresses, "Remember that your bird should have no other model than the bat, because its membranes serve as an armour or rather means of binding together the pieces of its armour, that is the framework of the wings."

Though, of course, these designs could never hope to fly, Leonardo came closer to real success when, late in life, he sketched a man flying, clinging to a flat sheet, and therein provided the basic concept for the glider. "If a man takes a piece of canvas," he wrote, "treated with lime, 12 fathoms wide and of the same height, he can let himself fall from no matter what height, without coming to any harm." He also crowned his aeronautical research with the first designs for a parachute and for a helicopter, as M. J. B. Davy tells us in his *Interpretative History of Flight*:

> In addition to his statement of principles, Leonardo made two contributions to the science of aeronautics which may be regarded as wholly inventive in that there is no conclusive evidence that the underlying principles were earlier applied. He invented the parachute and the helicopter, illustrating the function of each in his notebooks. The latter represents the first *known* application of the screw, or helix, for use in the air. There is also some evidence to suggest that he invented, or at least anticipated, the invention of the balloon, for it is recorded that he made "figures" of thin wax which when filled with warm air rose in the air. If this was indeed the case, Leonardo anticipated the invention of the hot-air balloon, or Montgolfière, which took place in 1783, but there is no corroborative evidence of these experiments.

As I have indicated, the tragedy about Leonardo's work was that his sketches and notes remained unknown because of the foolishness of his executor, so that no one was in a position to experiment with—and improve on—them for nearly three hundred years. If this had been otherwise, the whole course of aeronautical history would surely have been changed. Only the spirit of what he was trying to achieve—and the oral tales about his work which certainly spread across Italy, if not further afield—remained to act as a spur to other would-be birdmen over the intervening years.

While Leonardo was still drawing and speculating, other Italians were already definitely carrying out aerial experiments with artificial wings. Perhaps the foremost of these was Giovanni Baptiste Danti, a mathematician and engineer from the town of Perugia.

Recent commentators have speculated as to whether Leonardo and Danti knew each other, perhaps even discussed their ideas together. On the surface it seems unlikely— Leonardo was loath to share his thoughts with anyone—but on the other hand he could hardly have failed to hear of Danti's attempts to fly across Lake Trasimeno which were widely talked about in 1490 and thereafter. And who was it that had suggested tests should be carried out over water?

Danti, who lived from 1477 to 1517, was a wealthy, educated man, much admired by his contemporaries, and it is no surprise to find that no less than four chroniclers record his aerial endeavours. The most evocative account is that given by Cesare Alessi in his *Elogia Civium Perusinorum* (1652):

> A man to induce astonished admiration was Giovanni Baptiste Danti, the Daedalus of Perugia, who, after he had worked hard at mathematical studies, made among many other such things of his own devising, a pair of wings, properly proportioned to his body, which he fixed to himself with the skill of a man of the greatest mechanical genius. Having arranged these so as to produce effective flight, he several times tried them out over Lake Trasimeno. As soon as they responded perfectly to his control, he decided to try them publicly in Perugia.
>
> And when in that town a great gathering of eminent people was assembled for the nuptials of the Sister of Giampaolo Baglioni, who was being given in marriage to the most valiant Duke Bartholommeo Alviano, and when a crowd of people were gathered in the great square for jousting, behold, suddenly there was Danti, flying through the air from a high part of the city with a great rushing sound, enveloped in various kinds of feathers, crossing from one side to the other of the square with his great pair of wings, so astonishing everyone, and indeed terrifying quite a few, that they thought they were witnessing to some great and portentous monster.

But when, having left the low earth behind, he was trying with his proud limbs to attain through the high air the summit of his genius, envious Fortune, indignant at so much audacity, broke the iron bar which controlled the left wing, and as Danti could not sustain the weight of his body with the help of the other wing alone, he fell heavily on to the roof of the Church of St Mary, and to his great distress, and that of everyone, hurt his leg. After he had recovered, Giampaolo Baglioni took him to Venice as his mathematician, distinguishing him both with honours and a large stipend.

Another description of Danti, by Cesare Crispolti in the *Perugia Augusta* (1648), is rather more detailed in the description of the birdman's 'wings'. It has led scholars to believe that he wore two wings fixed rigidly by an iron pole, functioning something like a glider, and which would in all likelihood have enabled him to swoop to the ground from a high point rather than plunge straight down—was the usual fate of birdmen at this time. After his crash on the church roof—which resulted in a broken thigh—Danti seems to have rested on his laurels and consigned his feathered birdman suit and wings to the wardrobe.

Another Italian contemporary of Leonardo and Danti also took to the air on wings in 1507, but far away from those sunny climes. He chose a cold September morning in Scotland. This birdman was John Damian, a clever confidence trickster, who appears to have beguiled people of all ranks alike out of their money and land. Like Danti, too, he might have been inspired by the stories of Leonardo's experiments.

Damian seems to have arrived in Scotland in 1501; he had previously been in France and Italy (and had probably been sent packing—or been forced to flee from these countries—because of his devious ways). Nonetheless, he quickly ingratiated himself with James IV, who was taken by his "merry nature" and ignored the advice of his courtiers that the Italian was simply planning to scheme men out of their property. So silver-tongued was he, indeed, that he convinced the King he was a skilful physician and alchemist, and by 1504 had got himself elevated to the position of Abbot of Tungland.

But while Damian had the King's ear, he sensed he was universally disliked by the other nobles—who disbelieved all his claims—and therefore decided to demonstrate his powers by showing that he could fly.

On the morning of 27th September 1507, when the King was at Stirling Castle and had just despatched an ambassador to France, Damian announced that he would put on wings and arrive in Paris before the man. Bishop John Lesley in his *Historie of Scotland* (c 1568) recounts that "he causet mak ane pair of wingis of fedderis, quhilkis beand fessinit apoun him, he flew of the castell wall of Striveling, bot shortlie he fell to the ground and brak his thee bane".

The quick-witted Damian was not lost for a reason for his failure when the King reached his side. His wings, he explained,

> were composed of various feathers; among them were the feathers of a dunghill fowl, and they, by a certain sympathy, were attracted to the dunghill on which I fell; whereas, had my wings been composed of eagles alone, as I proposed, the same sympathy would have attracted my machine to the higher regions of the air.

James's favour continued to shine on Damian unabated, much to the chagrin of the other nobles who felt the aerial downfall might have meant his worldly downfall, too. Only a satire by William Dunbar, the Scottish poet, in which he attributed Damian's fall to his being set upon by savage birds, who resented his intrusion into their domain, assuaged their frustration and anger to any degree.

Despite his scheming nature and the unfortunate use of hens' feathers for his wings—it was the universal conviction of the time that only the feathers of powerful soaring birds would enable a man to fly—there can be little doubt that Damian was convinced manflight was possible, and thereby earns a place in history for his daring, if not his morality.

Other Italians, also doubtless inspired by tales of Leonardo and the other birdmen, were taking to the wing and should be mentioned briefly here.

The first of these—whose name unfortunately is not recorded—was another man like Damian who sought to exploit his 'skill' abroad: in this instance, in France at some time around 1580. Our reporter is the French poet, Augie Gaillard, who wrote somewhat mockingly about the attempt in his *Lou Banquet d'Augie Gaillard* (1583).

This "dolt of an Italian", as the poet called the birdman, said that he had built a pair of wings which he would use to fly "like a turtle dove" from the Tour de Nesles to the Tour du Grand Prévôt in Paris. His wings were apparently made of cloth on a rigid frame under which he hung. On the day of the attempt over five hundred thousand people assembled in the vicinity of the Tour. However, says Gaillard, when the Italian launched himself, "he dropped like a pig close to the base of the tower and broke his neck".

A second man, Paolo Guidotti, seems to have set out to imitate Leonardo, but suffered from the same defects of character as John Damian. Guidotti, who was born in Lucca in 1569, was a painter, sculptor and poet, but because of his liking for the high life and his unstable character was considered a charlatan by many people. Nevertheless, he was a man with an intensely enquiring mind, and though he frequently abandoned projects before their completion, seems to have given much time and thought to flight, and put into practice some of Leonardo's theories. After being in Rome for a few years he decided about 1595 to attempt a flight, as F. Baldinucci describes in *Notizie de'Professori del Disegno* (1681):

> Paolo took it into his head that he could discover how to fly, and with great ingenuity and labour he made wings from whalebone covered with feathers, giving them curvature by means of springs. He fixed them under his arms so that he might also use them in raising the wings during the act of flight, and after he had made many trials, he finally put himself to the test, throwing himself from a height and, with the help of the wings, carried himself forward for about a quarter of a mile, not, in my view, flying, but falling more slowly than he would have done without the wings.
>
> This, then, is what Guidotti did, who, finally tired with the fatigue of moving his arms, fell onto a roof, which broke, and he, dropping through a hole, found himself in the room beneath, gaining from his flight a broken thigh which left him in a sorry plight.

Modern commentators have disputed some elements of this report, in particular the distance which Guidotti is said to have flown, but all seem satisfied that a sustained glide, if only of modest distance, was achieved by this remarkable

The extraordinary hand-operated "flying wing" which features in Ralph Morris's account of *The Adventures of John Daniel* (1751)

he engraving which
companied Richard
wen Cambridge's
roic poem
Cribleriad" (1751)

Two illustrations from Robert Paltock's inventive novel of a race of winged people, *The Adventures of Peter Wilkins* (1763): the first shows one of the women, a Gawrey, preparing her wings for flight; the second, two men – or Glums – engaged in an aerial battle

(*above*) Two illustrations from one of the most famous novels about winged men – Restif de la Bretonne's *La Decouverte Australe par un Homme-volant*. The flying man tries out his wings and, having mastered the skill, carries off the object of his affections to a new life

(*right*) "The Attempt of the Mechanist to Use his Wings" – an engraving from Samuel Johnson's *Rasselas* (1759)

An illustrated sheet sold as a poster by a French publisher to cash in on the tremendous public interest in flight. Included are both man-powered and engine-powered machines

AVIATION

E SUR LA NAVIGATION AÉRIENNE SANS BALLONS

Dʳ HUREAU DE VILLENEUVE

Nota. — Les appareils précédés du signe * ont été construits et expérimentés.

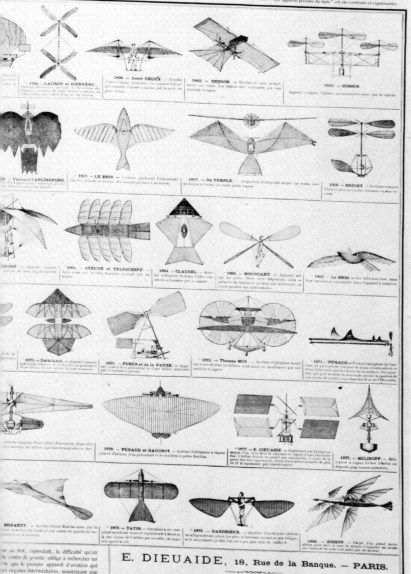

A rare sketch of the flying machine designed by the Italian philosopher and scientist Francesco Lana in 1670

The elderly Marquis de Bacqueville who attempted to fly across the River Seine in 1742

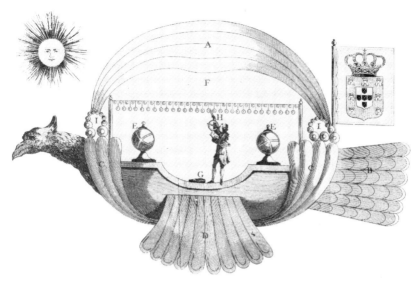

A highly fanciful interpretation of the "Passarola" of Father Laurenco de Gusmao, a model of which is said to have flown before the King of Portugal in 1709. (*below*) The German architect Carl Meerwin with the huge wings which some experts think may have allowed him to glide for a short distance

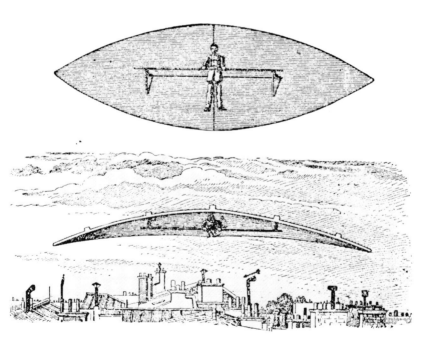

All the aerial exploits of the eighteenth century provided the cartoonists with excellent material. In these two French engravings an ingenious method of flight has been devised where would-be fliers are simply pumped full of air!

l'Aéromanie ou l'Art de voyager dans l'air decouvert en 1783.

A. Les Adieux éternels.
B. Maître de poste, tenant l'air inflammable.
C. Voyageurs attendent le Clistere.
D. Voyageurs en route.
E. Voyageur allant retenir sa place.
F. Commis.

The English humourists were a little less vulgar than their French counterparts, but equally ingenious. These two views of "Aerial Philosophers" were best-selling prints in Britain for years

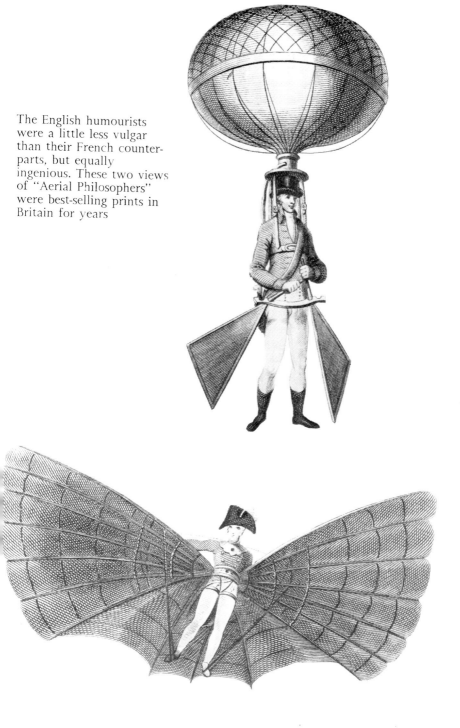

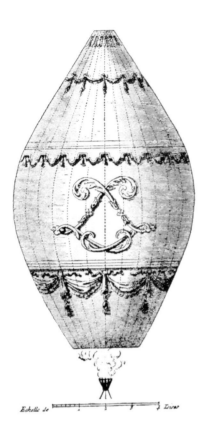

The first experimental balloon of the Montgolfier brothers, which led to their successful flight

(*below left*) Jean Blanchard with his "flying ship" worked by levers. He was only able to fly in this machine with the aid of a balloon. (*right*) A detailed illustration of the wings and harness used by the French experimenter Resnier de Goué in 1801

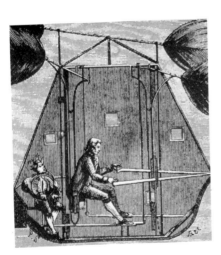

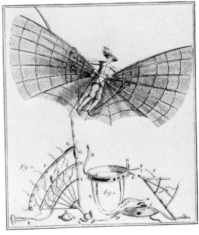

The end of the flight of the luckless "Tailor of Ulm" – in the Danube in 1811. From a German engraving

(*below*) The Swiss clockmaker Jacob Degen with the wings he used in conjunction with a balloon to give flying demonstrations – although the ballon is not shown in this publicity picture

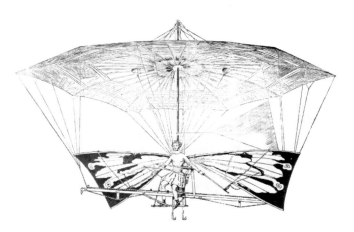

The contrivance, a cross between a parachute and a glider, designed by the Frenchman L. C. Letur in 1853

Sir George Cayley, the English nobleman who progressed from experiments with crude gliders to proposing the first practicable powered aeroplane in 1809 (a still from *Conquest of the Air*)

The detailed drawing for W. Miller's "Aerostat" which was published in 1843. How close to the modern hang-glider this device seems!

Another anonymous design based on the Miller "Aerostat" and published as a print for public sale in 1845

One of the first photographs in aeronautical history: the huge glider built to resemble an albatross by the French sea captain and inventor J. M. le Bris in 1857

Illustration from the *Chronique Industrielle* of Monsieur A. Goupil's "aerial velocipede"

A newspaper sketch of one of the early American birdmen, W. P. Quimby, who tried to fly with this curious equipment in the 1870s

The "Improved Airship" of John Holmes of Kansas – an interesting use of the idea of pedal-power

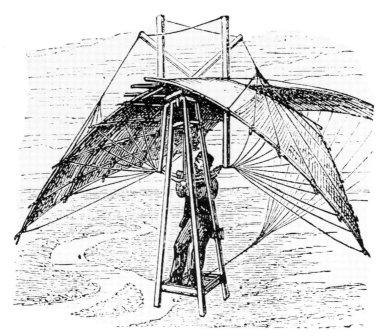

The amazing flapping machine designed by the Belgian Vincent de Groof, in which he gave exhibitions. He was raised into the sky by a balloon and then released to descend partly by gliding and partly by flapping the large wings. Tragically, his wings collapsed under the air pressure when he was giving a display over London, and he crashed to his death

The man who made soaring flight a reality – the German pioneer Otto Lilienthal. (*below*) Lilienthal photographed in the last soaring machine he developed – and the one in which he died in 1896. (*bottom*) Lilienthal airborne in one of his impressive double-decker gliders

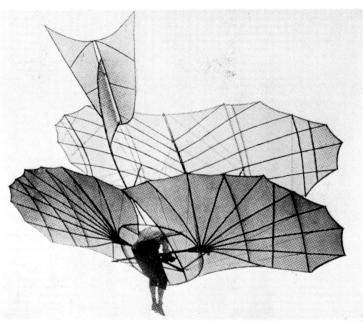

showman. Backed by Leonardo's speculation and his own daring, he had come within a wing and a prayer of flight.

A final Italian story, related by Johannes Sturm in his *Lingra Latinae Resoluendae Ratio* at the end of the sixteenth century, tells of a completely successful flight by a birdman who jumped from the tower of St Mark's in Venice and "circled and swooped above the heads of the amazed population who felt for certain that he was an angel of God until his wings brought him safely again to earth". As no documented facts have ever been produced about this story—and Sturm was renowned for using evocative episodes of fiction to underline his philosophizing—its truth seems highly improbable.

It was a story, though, that spread far and wide throughout Europe—magnified in some quarters by politicians who feared Italian mastery of the air, and admired by others as typifying the desire everyone had for flight. One man who studied it and made a particular point about the valour of the aeronaut was the English bishop John Wilkins, who was to play an important role in the great upsurge in the number of attempted man-powered flights in the seventeenth century. For the lead Leonardo and his Italians had given was to have far-reaching effects on the rest of Europe in the years to come. . . .

[6]

A Flurry of Birdmen

The possibility of flight by means of artificial wings undoubtedly dominated the minds of experimenters, both scientists and laymen, throughout the seventeenth century. In
earlier centuries, a substantial number of daring birdmen had
leapt into history—some whose names and activities we are
aware of, others who are forgotten, though all remain banded
together as those who had the courage of their conviction
that one day man must fly—but it was in the seventeenth
century that, not daunted by the catalogue of serious injury
and deaths already existing, the most concerted efforts took
place. That they proved a stepping-stone towards the balloon,
the glider and, eventually, the aeroplane, stresses their importance.

Just as one man, Leonardo, had dominated thought in the
sixteenth century, so was another single voice to stimulate
popular interest in flight in the seventeenth: John Wilkins,
the Bishop of Chester, who lived from 1614 to 1672. Wilkins,
a quiet, gentle and religious man, became, as a result of his
aeronautical writings, "for a time, and to his acute embarrass-
ment, the most popular man of letters of the day and a lion
among the ladies" according to Marjorie Hope Nicolson in
her *Voyages to the Moon* (1948). She adds: "And rumour had
it that Wilkins had already found the answer to the great
enigma."

Wilkins was born at Daventry and obtained a B.A. at
Oxford before entering the Church as a chaplain. From an
early age he had been interested in science and with spare
time at his disposal outside his ecclesiastical duties, took up
a wide-ranging study of the subject. An early and profound
influence on him was Roger Bacon, and it was his references

to flight, plus reading one of the earliest fantasy novels, *The Man in the Moone, or a Discourse of a Voyage thither by Domingo Gonsales the Speedy Messenger*, written by Francis Godwin and published in 1638, which ignited his life-long fascination with aeronautics. (Godwin, who was the Bishop of Hereford, only dealt with flying in a fictional form and we shall discuss his importance in our history in the next chapter.)

Wilkins's first publication, *Discovery of a New World* which appeared late in 1638, took up Godwin's theme of the moon—which he believed was habitable—and the means by which man might reach it. Wilkins was convinced that if a man could fly as high as twenty miles he would overcome the earth's magnetism and become weightless, and could then move freely wherever he wanted in space. In a second work, *Discourse concerning the Possibility of a Passage to the World in the Moon* (1640) he advocated a "cup or wooden vessel" filled with fire or ethereal air which he believed could convey man to any height he desired.

In these two books he also touched upon the birdman concept, writing in the first instance:

> It is the most obvious and common opinion that this may be effected by wings fastened immediately to the body, this coming nearest to the imitation of nature, which should be observed in such attempts as these. This is the way which Fredericus Hermannus, in his little discourse, *De Arte Volandi*, doth only mention and insist upon; and if we may trust credible story, it hath been frequently attempted not without success.

Like his mentor Bacon, Wilkins was intensely optimistic about human potential, and believed the greatest obstacle to progress was that man convinced himself that things were impossible without even trying them. He knew that experience had been costly to the birdmen in terms of human suffering, but wrote thus in a resounding paragraph—the last sentence based on actual incident—which was echoed by scientific experiment and literature for a century thereafter:

> Though the truth is, most of these artists did unfortunately miscarry by falling down, and breaking their arms and legs, yet that may be imputed to their want of experience, and too much fear, which needs must possess men in such dangerous

and strange attempts. Those things that seem very difficult and fearful at the first, may grow very facile after frequent trial and exercise. And therefore he that would effect anything in this kind, must be brought up to the constant practice of it from his youth. Trying first only to use his wings in running on the ground, as an ostrich or tame goose would do, touching the earth with his toes; and so by degrees learn to rise higher, till he shall attain unto skill and confidence. I have heard it from credible testimony, that one of our own nation hath proceeded so far in this experiment, that he was able by the help of wings in such a running pace, to step constantly ten yards at a time.

Wilkins's two books—"among the earliest printed works in which the subject of flight is considered and discussed as a scientific problem" to quote M. J. B. Davy—were followed by his masterpiece, *Mathematical Magick*, which was published in 1648 and developed the theme of man-powered flight still further. First, Wilkins gave a resumé of previous attempts, analysed them in a scientific manner, and suggested that as the arms were obviously not strong enough to effect flight un-aided, why then the legs should be given wings, too.

It is worth the inquiry [he wrote], to consider whether this might not be more probably effected by the labour of the feet, which are naturally more strong and indefatigable: in which contrivance the wings should come down from the shoulders on each side, as in the other, but the motion of them should be from the legs being thrust out, and drawn in again one after another, so as each leg should move both wings; by which means a man should (as it were) walk or climb up into the air; and then the hands and arms might be at leisure to help and direct the motion, or for any other service proportionable to their strength. Which conjecture is not without good proba-bility, and some especial advantages above the other.

While Wilkins's suggestion certainly had "advantages" over previous wings, it was, of course, as doomed to failure as all the rest. The importance of what he had said, in fact, lay not in his theories, but in his convincing argument that success was possible, and in his scientific approach, which caused his books to be widely read and to give rise to great discussion about the principles involved in flying. (Bishop Wilkins also made proposals for a "flying chariot" in which he gave a true exposition of the lighter-than-air principle, and stressed the importance of studying gliding flight as another step towards the conquest of the air: both points which further underline his stature in the realm of aeronautics and for which the later pioneer balloonists and glider pilots had to thank him.)

A certain Robert Hooke, an English contemporary of Bishop Wilkins—and for some years a friend of his—was also deeply immersed in the problems of flight. Indeed, some later historians have claimed more importance in the history of artificial wings for him than for the gentle clergyman from Chester. Of this enigmatic man the diarist Samuel Pepys wrote, "Mr Hooke is the most, and promises the least, of any man in the world that ever I saw".

Hooke, who was born in 1635, showed himself to be a first-class scientist, expert craftsman and superb draughtsman, and soon proved one of the leading lights of the Royal Society after it was revived in 1660. Here it was that he met Wilkins and the two men had long and earnest discussions about their mutual passion.

Hooke, however, had been experimenting from at least 1655, and, in contrast to Wilkins, was convinced the human body was not strong enough to power artificial wings. In his study, *Micrographia*, he summarized:

> The way of flying in the air seems principally impracticable by reason of the want of strength in human Muscles; if therefore that could be supplied, it were, I think, easier to make twenty contrivances to perform the offices of wings.

In 1660 he told members of the new Royal Society that he had "made many trials about the Art of Flying in the Air, and moving very swiftly on the Land and Water". He reported that he had made a model which, by means of springs and wings, raised and supported itself in the air, but when it came to adapting his design to human flight he again faced the problem of "the want of strength in human muscles".

Another Royal Society member with whom Hooke discussed the problem was Christopher Wren, the architect who later designed St Paul's Cathedral. Like Hooke, Wren appears to have delivered lectures to the organization stressing that a machine of some kind was needed to raise man from the ground, but he had no specific design to offer.

In February 1675, however, Hooke made his most tantalizing announcement when—according to the Society's records—he "intimated that there was a way which he knew, to produce strength, so as to give to one man the strength of ten or twenty or more, and to contrive muscles for him of an equivalent strength to those in birds". He hinted, likewise, that "a contrivance might be made of something more proper for the feet of man to tread the air, than for his arms to beat the air".

Thus far he went, and no farther. Later, editing his papers for publication, another Royal Society member, Richard Waller, said that he had seen sketches by Hooke which showed a craft resembling a helicopter which would raise a man "by means of horizontal vanes placed a little aslope to the wind". If only one of these drawings had survived to the present day, it might be possible to establish whether or not Hooke did construct and fly some kind of primitive ornithopter or helicopter.

Throughout his life, Hooke was just as fascinated with other's attempts to fly as he was with his own experiments—indeed, his notebooks, kept religiously until his death in 1703, detailed most of the attempted flights which we shall discuss in the remainder of this section. As he wrote at the turn of the century,

> We have not wanted later instances in England and elsewhere of several ingenious men who have employed their wits and time about this design. Particularly, I have been credibly informed, that one Mr Gascoigne did about 40 years since try it with good effect, though he since dying, the thing also died with him. And even now, there are not wanting some in England who affirm themselves able to do it, and that they have proved as much by experiment. We have little or no account of the ways they have taken to effect their designs; but we may conclude them defective in somewhat or other, since we do not find them brought into common use.

Of Mr Gascoigne and those others "in England" to whom Hooke refers, no details other than this brief mention have survived; we are, though, more fortunate concerning places farther afield. The obsession with flying which had so gripped Wilkins and Hooke was similarly spread throughout Europe and resulted in a "veritable flurry of birdmen" as a writer in the *Annual Register* for 1678 so aptly put it.

Russian mythology and legend is as full of winged gods and heroes as that of any other nation, and indeed her recorded history is also dotted with occasional accounts of men attempting flight with wings or suits of cloth. Stories of several of these attempts remain untranslated and extremely difficult to locate (probably justifiably so, since their scanty detail has led historians to describe them as "highly improbable"). There is, however, a fairly well authenticated story about a birdman during the reign of Ivan the Terrible (Ivan IV, 1530–1584). Ivan, whose mental balance was apparently affected by the death of his first wife in 1560, had brought before him a man who tried flying from a building wearing wings of wood and cloth. The ruler is said to have been thrown into a rage by the man's endeavours and to have sentenced him to death on the grounds that "attempting to quit the confines of the earth was a gross and unnatural act".

In seventeenth-century Russia there were three interesting reports. The first dates from 1610 when a would-be birdman named Vliskov jumped from a high building in Moscow, clad in wings "made from feathers of eagles and a suit of folded linen". This combination of feathers and linen is not previously recorded in our history, and though the birdman is said to have plunged fairly swiftly to the ground, "the feathers and cloth restricted his injuries to bruising and cuts".

In the 1630s a prisoner escaped from a Russian fortress near the Black Sea by using a pair of wings he had secretly manufactured from stolen wood and the linen of his bed. The account says he dived off a high rampart late one night, landing in a forest nearby, but was so exhausted by his labours that he was easily caught by the pursuing guards and their dogs. So amazed were the authorities by his ingenuity, however, that they forced him to repeat his exploit. Once again he leapt from the rampart, but this time he only drifted about fifteen yards and landed beside a stake used in the execution of criminals. To the superstitious guards, this seemed like an omen that the man obtained his power to fly by supernatural means—so they condemned him as a sorcerer and burnt him at that very stake.

The third story again concerns an anonymous Russian, this time a Ukrainian peasant, who apparently believed he could fly and boasted of this to all and sundry. When word of the man's claim reached the ears of the nobleman in whose province he lived, he was summoned to appear before a special assembly and demonstrate his skill. Dressed in his wings made of wax and feathers, says an account, and surrounded by a crowd of gaping peasants and the entourage of his master, the hapless man flapped his wings and jumped vainly up and down trying to take off from the ground. When he finally sank exhausted and defeated to the ground, he was awarded a whipping for his foolishness.

The Russians, a practical people if ever there was one, seem to have lost interest in the idea of man-powered flight shortly after this—certainly there are no more birdmen stories—but once the age of actual flight dawned, they were as quick and progressive in its development as anyone else: culminating, of course, in their being the first to send a man into space. (They have recently, though, begun to look again at the subject of man-powered flight in relation to insects, as I report in Chapter 10.)

But to return to the seventeenth century. In Turkey we find a strong claim for a successful flight by one Hezarfen Celebi sometime around the middle of the century. He is said to have launched himself from a tower in Galatia, on the shores of the Bosphorus, and winged his way for "several kilometres". He finally landed safely, so the story goes, in the market place at Scutari, where his triumph "made him the most fêted man in all Turkey while he was alive". Celebi apparently never attempted to repeat his flight and no exact detail of the construction of his wings has survived.

This particular story has interested a number of experts over the years, including John W. R. Taylor, the authoritative editor of *Jane's All the World's Aircraft*, who told me recently,

There are several authorities who claim this to be one of the very few successful birdmen flights. The Turks certainly believe he flew. They even issued a postage stamp at the time of the Istanbul Civil Aviation Congress of 1950, showing him shortly after take-off. (Illustrated elsewhere).

If Celebi's 'aircraft' really was anything like that shown on the stamp, it might have had sufficient wing area to carry him the distance claimed, provided he kept the wings rigid and did not try to flap them. But we shall never know for certain whether this gallant Turk deserves more credit than he gets in the average aviation book.

In 1648, in Poland, we come across one of the few records of an actual model aircraft being built at this time. The story concerns a man named Tito Burattini, who was born in Venice in 1615, but settled in Poland some time in the early 1640s. He was apparently obsessed with the idea of flight and first built a miniature flying machine, worked by springs, which had four pairs of wings in tandem—the two middle pairs for lifting, the bow pair for propulsion, and the stern pair for propulsion and lift—and a tail unit which was used for direction. He tested this with a cat as the passenger and it is said to have risen several yards into the air. Encouraged by his success, he next made a full-size version, which he personally tested in 1648. Details of the exploit are scant and seem to indicate that Burattini may have left the ground, but his "flying dragon", as he called the machine, almost immediately crashed and was completely wrecked. There is, though, much conjecture about this claim, and it has been suggested that the Venetian's "dragon" may only have been a large kite, which was distorted into a machine with the re-telling of the story in subsequent years!

The Germans seem to have been noticeably busy striving for flight during this century—their endeavours having been mainly inspired by the work of, once again, a religious man, Kaspar Mohr. Mohr, like Eilmer and others before him, not forgetting Leonardo, was a man of many parts: mathematician, sculptor, painter, carpenter, locksmith and clockmaker, as well as being a senior member of the Schussenried Monastery in Wurtemburg.

Mohr was born in 1575, and in 1610 left Germany to study theology in Rome, completing his doctorate in 1614. Returning home, he began to put some of his prodigious talents and learning to use in the construction of mechanical contrivances and was soon being hailed as a genius. But it was the idea of flight which particularly intrigued him and took up his labours in the monastery.

There, in the privacy of his cell, he made a pair of wings from goose feathers fastened together over a frame with whipcord. Reports have it that he practised in secret with these wings for many months before finally believing he was ready to attempt a flight. However, word seems to have reached his superiors of the plan, and on the night he planned to jump from the top of the three-storey dormitory of the monastery, his wings were confiscated and he was forbidden to make any such attempts.

B. Wilhelm, writing in his study *Schweikart und Mohr* (1909), believes that the monk was prevented from flying not because it was thought he would fail, but simply to make him direct his genius to other more relevant topics. There was every faith in his skill, the more so because he was said to have learned much about it when in Italy by studying Leonardo's work and the attempts of Danti and Guidotti. There is a report that Mohr later defied his superiors and, having made a second set of wings, took off from the dormitory one night and flew for nearly two hours! This story has subsequently proved impossible to substantiate and most authorities are inclined to dismiss it entirely. In any event, after his death in June 1625, this undoubted pioneer of flight was commemorated by a painting of himself and his wings on the ceiling of the library in the Schussenried Monastery, which survives to this day.

At about the time of the confiscation of Mohr's wings, a man known as Senecio is said to have attempted to fly at Nuremburg. This man, who was a cantor and probably quite elderly, came to an unhappy fate, as the historian J. E. Burggravius tells us in *Achilles Redivivus* (1612):

> This man, having risen into the air by the help of wings, or by means of some beating arrangement, flew here and there, and then, like a bird of omen, descended once more. But even so, having fallen at last owing to some error which caused the little wheels, of what kind I do not know, to which the wings were fixed and which made the flight possible, to become either distorted or improperly applied, and rendered powerless, he, having been thrown to the ground, broke his arms and legs.

The details of the birdman's equipment have intrigued several experts—as, indeed, has his alleged success at such an advanced age—but unfortunately no specific details or sketch has survived.

Nuremburg seems to have been something of a hotbed for

would-be aviators at this period, for there are also reported attempts at flight by an unnamed man in 1630 (which ended in his death) and by a mechanic and inventor named Hautsch shortly thereafter. Hautsch was said to have built a "flying machine" among the several other inventions which made him celebrated throughout Germany in the middle years of the seventeenth century. Unfortunately, later study has discredited much that Hautsch claimed and this is probably also true of his flying machine.

A final German attempt at this time is recorded in 1673 when a man named Bernoin jumped from the walls of a high building in Frankfurt. He plunged to the ground and broke both his neck and his legs. This was perhaps a sad end to so much endeavour after the Germans had come so close to success. Nevertheless, it was a German, Otto Lilienthal, who, as we shall see later, reaped the reward of his countrymen's courage when his development of the glider led directly to the flight of the Wright brothers.

The French, too, were busy experimenting in this area, and had been inspired by the work of Leonardo and the Italians like the clockmaker, Bolori, who in 1536, visited the country and attempted to fly from the cathedral at Troyes, but paid for his daring with his life.

The earliest of the local birdmen seems to have been a man named Alard, who in about 1660 claimed that he would give a demonstration of his skill before Louis XIV. Alard was apparently a rope-dancer who earned his livelihood by walking across high wires and juggling. He planned to augment this feat—and his purse—by donning wings which he would then use to fly from the terrace of Saint Germain to the woods of Le Vesinet. Having gained the height he needed for take-off on his rope, he struck out with his wings, but immediately plunged down and was seriously hurt.

In France there are also a number of other reports of rope-dancers like Alard who claimed they could fly, but in retrospect historians believe that these are mostly distortions of the truth: the very walking on a high wire was seen by many people as a kind of 'flight', and subsequently men were said to have flown when their nimble feet never left the rope.

The religious community was also busy attempting to fly, and we have a report of the learned Canon Oger of Rosoy

Abbey who built himself a pair of wings, but when he leapt from the abbey roof was lucky enough to fall into a bush and thereby save his life. At Peronne, another priest, wearing cloth and feather wings, was also saved from injury when he fell into a moat.

The most famous and inventive of the French birdmen was undoubtedly a locksmith named Besnier who attempted to fly at Sable in 1678. His attempt also became the most widely discussed single aeronautical event of the century.

Besnier, unlike his contemporaries, based his flying apparatus on a principle similar to that of the water-bird's webbed feet. His machine consisted of four wings, or paddles, mounted at the ends of levers, which rested on the shoulders of the man who guided it; he could move them alternately by means of his hands and feet (see opposite). The 'wings' at the ends of the poles were, said Besnier, "an oblong chassie of taffety, which chassies fold from above downward."

This birdman apparently made a number of secret trials with his invention on the roofs of Paris before making an actual attempt at flight which was described in the 12th December 1678 issue of the *Journal de Paris*:

> The 'wings' of M. Besnier are oblong frames, covered with taffeta, and attached to the ends of two rods, adjusted on the shoulders. The wings work up and down. Those in front are worked by the hands; those behind by the feet, which are connected with the ends of the rods by strings. The movements were such that when the right hand made the right wing descend in front the left foot made the left wing descend behind; and in like manner the left hand in front and the right foot behind acted together simultaneously. This diagonal action appeared very well contrived; it was the action of most quadrupeds as well as of man when walking; but the contrivance, like others of the same kind, failed in not being fitted with gearing to enable the air traveller to proceed in any other direction than that in which the wind blew him. The inventor first flew down from a stool, then from a table, afterwards from a window, and finally from a garret, from which he passed above the houses in the neighbourhood, and then, moderating the working of his machine, he descended slowly to earth.

Naturally, this report and others emanating from the French press—the majority of which were highly sceptical about

Besnier's success—caused great excitement and controversy. In England, the industrious Robert Hooke was immediately fascinated by the story and, based on the reports, produced a model of the contrivance and an explanatory diagram for his fellow members of the Royal Society. Both the diagram and

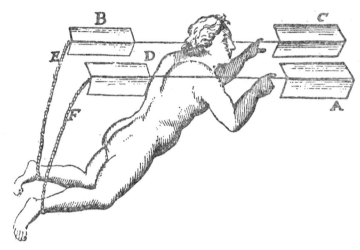

Robert Hooke's diagram illustrating Besnier's flying equipment

Hooke's text still exist in the *Philosophical Transactions* and the preamble reads:

The Art of Flying: by S. Besnier. The Sieur Besnier, a smith of Sable in the County of Maine, hath invented an Engine for Flying. It consists of two Poles or Rods, which have at each end of them an oblong Chassie of Taffety; with Chassie folds from above downwards, as the frame of a folding Window Chassie. He sits these Poles upon his Shoulders, so that two of the Chassies may be before him, and the other two behind him. The order of moving them is this: When the Right Hand strikes down the right Wing before, A, the left leg by means of the String E, pulls downwards the left Wing behind, B; then immediately after the left Hand moves or strikes downwards the left Wing before, C; and at the same time the right Foot, by the String E, moves or pulls down the right Wing behind D; and so successively or alternately, the diagonally opposite Wings always moving downwards, or striking the Air together.

This story has continued to fascinate experts ever since, and one summarized recently:

> Besnier is said to have made careful experiments and finally soared over a house and landed safely; this probably means he descended from the roof of the house. The apparatus he used must clearly have been more sophisticated and many times larger than that shown, which is a concept similar to that of the flap-valve. It would just be possible for a man to make a floundering glide without coming to grief, if the 'machine' parachuted him down, which would seem to be the explanation of those survivals and maiming with which fortune favoured a few.

Marjorie Hope Nicolson has also written in her *Voyages to the Moon*:

> The invention of the French smith, which seems to have been an attempt to combine wings with the principle of the parachute, suggests that flyers of the seventeenth century had already proceeded far beyond those early experimenters from Bladud to Damian whose conception of wings was limited to feathers attached only to the arms. Though Besnier's invention was crude and his flight short, enthusiasts of aviation worked for years upon improvements to his principle.

However, if Besnier's attempt was to inspire later aeronauts, an Italian professor struck a blow at the hopes of all those generations of birdmen who believed man would fly with wings powered by his own muscles. Just as his fellow countryman Leonardo had opened up the possibilities in this area, so Giovanni Alphonso Borelli, the professor of mathematics at Messina, finally spelt out the basic limitations.

Borelli, who lived from 1608 to 1679, made a long and arduous study of flight before publishing his critical treatise *De Motu Animalium* in Rome in 1680. In this he proved conclusively that because of the inadequate power and weight of human muscles in comparison to those of a bird, "it is impossible that men should be able to fly craftily by their own strength". Borelli's study contained a reasoned analysis of flight with the relevant statistics, and—though a shattering blow to his contemporaries—was a milestone in the history of aviation. There now seems little doubt that his conclusions were not at first wholly accepted—*vide* the further attempts by birdmen in the eighteenth century—but his logic was irrefutable.

Today, of course, assisted by ultra-light materials and backed up by advanced knowledge of aerodynamics, man-powered flight is feasible. But this is only a very modern development, and in the light of hindsight, Borelli's shattering of so many hopes and dreams brought a timely end to many accidents to life and limb in attempts to fly.

All the endeavour had not been wasted, though, for man was now on the verge of understanding that while he would never fly by flapping wings, he might ride the air on a rigid wing or glider. If he could only have appreciated the need to stabilize such flight by a tail, conquest of the air would almost certainly have been in his grasp a century and a half earlier than it actually was. "It is thus understandable," M. J. B. Davy has written, "that the eighteenth century was almost devoid of actual experiment in regard to mechanical flight, and that when an alternative method of aerial navigation presented itself, it was eagerly grasped and exploited."

Before making this big jump in history, however, I think we should look at some of the works of literature which were published in the seventeenth and eighteenth century, as this was—to quote Henry Coxwell—"the time *par excellence* for narratives of imaginary travels. For it was then that the exploits of the birdmen and the great advances in astronomy had opened up a new world of marvels".

[7]

Flights of Fancy

The books about 'cosmic voyages' on wings or in strange machines which appeared in number in the seventeenth and eighteenth centuries were inspired by several factors: the legends and tales of Icarus, Bladud, Damian and company; the experiments and theories of Roger Bacon and Leonardo; and a mixture of classic literature and new science. All these elements appeared to a varying degree in this new literature of flight and found a voracious and enthusiastic readership throughout Europe.

The recent great advances, in astronomy particularly, had shown that the old romances (such as those by Lucian, Plutarch and Cicero and the medieval writers) about worlds beyond our own were not so fantastic as had previously been imagined. Observers were now able to *see* the surface of the moon, distinguish many other heavenly bodies, and determine that, far from being at the centre of things, the earth was merely a tiny speck in a vast and awe-inspiring universe. Here indeed was food for speculation, and quickly following came the extraordinary narratives of excursions through space which embroidered on man's simple achievements towards flight and utilized certain basic scientific principles.

One of the first of these "travellers in imagination", as Henry Coxwell called them, was Francis Godwin, the Bishop of Hereford, who, as I mentioned in the previous chapter, was an important influence on John Wilkins, and later on Cyrano de Bergerac, Daniel Defoe and Jonathan Swift. Godwin, who was born in 1562, was the son of the Bishop of Bath and Wells, and, naturally enough, after graduating from Oxford, entered the Church. He was first Rector of Sampford, and then became Bishop of Hereford in 1617. Throughout his life he was interested in literature, writing several works on religion, but finding a place in history with his extraordinary fantasy, *The Man in the Moone, or a Discourse of a Voyage thither by Domingo Gonsales the Speedy Messenger*, which was published posthumously in 1638. (Godwin died in 1633.)

The *Voyage* describes how the Spaniard Gonsales flies to the moon with the aid of twenty-five trained geese. The birds are fixed to his conveyance by pulleys, and there is a sail at the front for direction. Gonsales himself sits on what can only be described as a trapeze bar and from there urges the birds upwards from their starting point on a mountain in Tenerife towards the moon; he arrives there safely twelve days later. Wilkins, as I have noted, utilized some of Godwin's fantasy for his *Discovery of a New World*.

A German contemporary of Godwin, Johann Kepler, an astronomer and mathematician, also wrote a fantasy about the moon and propounded—for the first time—lunar colonization. His work *Somnium* is a subject of some mystery, as the date of its composition has been impossible to authenticate. It seems highly unlikely that it was written before Godwin's *Man in the Moone*, particularly as scholars are now convinced that the Englishman composed his masterpiece while still a student at Oxford between 1578 and 1584. In any event, *Somnium* appeared in 1634, after Kepler had been dead four years following a sad series of events. According to Marjorie Hope Nicolson, Kepler, though a scientist, lived in an age of superstition and feared to publish his work during his lifetime, the more so because his mother had been condemned as a witch and would have been executed but for her son's courageous five-year fight on her behalf. Even the son-in-law to whom Kepler entrusted publication in his will died before actual copies came from the printer.

The book, in the form of a dream, describes how the central character—clearly modelled on the author—flies to the moon with supernatural aid, and what he finds there: including a gigantic race of serpentine creatures, some of which have limbs and others wings.

Somnium and the work of Godwin were both later parodied endlessly by other seventeenth-century writers, but there could be no denying the new realms of thought they had opened, and the fact that they established the genre of the moon voyage in fiction. Samuel Butler (in his *Elephant in the Moon*) and Henry More (in *Insomnium Philosophicum*) are two typical examples of parodies, although the latter does pay tribute to the more scientific elements of Kepler's work. It has been suggested, too, that John Milton's *Paradise Lost* may have been in part influenced by the German's strange and fantastic moon world.

Some authorities believe that the most brilliant of all the parodies are those of Cyrano de Bergerac (1619–55), the French writer and wit who is said to have fought more than a thousand duels as a result of insults about his large nose. Others contend that his works, such as *Histoire Comique des Etats de la Lune et du Soleil*, are simply superb *voyages imaginaires*. What is certain is that—while previous writers in the genre had been less than specific about the 'engines' of their aerial machines—Cyrano actually went into a kind of detail. As there is no space here to go into the voluminous description provided by the author, I shall let Henry Coxwell summarize as he does in his *Attempts to Fly in the Air*:

> Cyrano of Bergerac promulgates five different means of flying in the air. First, by means of phials filled with dew, which would attract and cause to mount up. Secondly, by a great bird made of wood, the wings of which should be kept in motion. Thirdly, by rockets, which, going off successively, would drive up the balloon by the force of projection. Fourthly, by an octahedron of glass, heated by the sun, and of which the lower part should be allowed to penetrate the dense cold air, which, pressing up against the rarefied hot air, would raise the balloon. Fifthly, by a car of iron and a ball of magnetized iron, which the aeronaut would keep throwing up in the air, and which would attract and draw up the balloon. The wiseacre who invented these modes of flying in the air seems, some would say, to have been more in want of very strict confinement on the earth than of the freedom of the skies.

Whatever the true intent of Cyrano's work, it certainly added fuel to the ever-growing fire of public interest in the mystery of flight, but although there were to be other advances in aeronautical design—which we shall mention in the next chapter—it was not until the advent of the eighteenth century that another major 'cosmic voyage' was published—Daniel Defoe's *Consolidator*, which appeared in 1705.

Defoe and his general work require no comment here, but his novel the *Consolidator* remains virtually unknown, although it is a superb account of a voyage to the moon. In it Defoe suggests that all the inventions of his day had, in fact, been known to ancient man, and discusses a Chinaman who had travelled to and from the moon many centuries earlier.

It has been claimed—though equally stoutly resisted—that in his work Defoe anticipated petrol, because his machine flew to the moon using a kind of fuel as the motive power. This is Defoe's description of his craft, the Consolidator of the title:

A certain Engine in the shape of a Chariot, on the backs of two vast Bodies with extended wings, which spread about fyfty yards in breadth, composed of Feathers so nicely put together that no air could pass; and as the Bodies were made of Lunar Earth, which would bear the Fire, the Cavities were filled with an ambient flame, which fed on a certain Spirit, deposited in a proper quantity to last out the voyage; and this Fire so ordered as to move about such springs and wheels as kept the wings in most exact and regular Motion, always ascendent.

Was this a brilliant piece of prophecy? Undoubtedly the flame "which fed on a certain Spirit" has no earlier mention in literature, and the fact that quantities had to be taken along to sustain the flight is an uncanny anticipation of the petrol age. The question is surely one for further study.

Once into the eighteenth century, the "literature of wings" becomes so prolific that only a mention of the more important works can be attempted. As Marjorie Hope Nicolson says, "There is much repetition, but little novelty among later authors. Satirists laughed, the more pessimistically inclined gloomily shook their heads, the optimists continued to believe that in time man would conquer the air. Major writers and minor all had their say on the subject." Let us consider some of them.

The essayist Joseph Addison probably best underlined the enthusiasm of the time with two satirical articles in the magazine the *Guardian* of 20th July 1713. In the first, which he signed himself, he speaks of all the advantages to be gained from the designs of "the famous Bishop Wilkins" and says it will not be long before "it will be as usual to hear a man call for his wings when he is going on a journey as it is now to call for his boots". In the second item, a letter said to be from an anonymous correspondent who signed himself "Daedalus", Addison took this theme still farther. He wrote:

Mr Ironside,

Knowing that you are a great encourager of ingenuity I think fit to acquaint you, that I have made a considerable progress in the art of flying. I flutter about my room two or three hours in the morning and when my wings are on, can go above a hundred yards at a hop, step, and jump. I can fly already as well as a Turkey-cock, and improve every day. If I proceed as well as I have begun, I intend to give the world a proof of my proficiency in this art. Upon the next public thanksgiving day, it is my design to sit astride the dragon upon Bow steeple, from whence, after the first discharge of the Tower guns, I intend to mount into the air, fly over Fleet Street, and pitch upon the May-pole in the Strand. From thence, by a gradual descent, I shall make the best of my way for St James's Park, and light upon the ground near Rosamund's pond. This, I doubt not, will convince the world, that I am no pretender; but before I set out, I shall have the desire to have a patent for making of wings, and that none shall presume to fly under pain of death, with wings of any other man's making. I intend to work for the court myself, and will have journeymen under me to furnish the rest of the nation. I likewise desire, that I may have the sole teaching of persons of quality, in which I shall spare neither time nor pains till I have made them as expert as myself. I will fly with the women upon my back for the first fortnight. I shall appear at the next masquerade, dressed up in my feathers and plumage like an Indian prince, that the quality may see how pretty they will look in their travelling habits. You know, sir, there is an unaccountable prejudice to projectors of all kinds, for which reason, when I talk of practising to fly silly people think me an owl for my pains; but sir, you know better things. I need not enumerate to you the benefits which accrue to the public from this invention, as how the roads of England will be saved when we travel through these new *high-ways*, and how all family accounts will be lessened in the article of coaches and horses. I need not mention post and packet-boats, with many other conveniences of life, which will be supplied in this way. In short, sir, when mankind are in possession of this art, they will be able to do more business in threescore and ten years, than they could do in a thousand by the methods now in use. I therefore recommend myself and my art to your patronage, and am,

Your most humble servant.

Addison could not, of course, resist a riposte to himself and, as "Mr Ironside", said he would use every method at his disposal to prevent man from flying in this manner.

It would fill the world [he wrote], with innumerable immoralities, and give such occasions for intrigues as people cannot meet with who have nothing but legs to carry them. You should have a couple of lovers make a midnight assignation upon the top of the Monument, and see the cupola of St Paul's covered with both sexes like the outside of a pigeon-house. Nothing would be more frequent than to see a beau flying in at a garret window, or a gallant giving chase to his mistress, like a hawk after a lark. There would be no walking in a shady wood without springing a covey of toasts. The poor husband could not dream what was doing over his head; if he were jealous, indeed, he might clip his wife's wings, but what would this avail when there were flocks of whore-masters perpetually hovering over his house? What concern would the father of a family be in all the time his daughter was upon the wing? Every heiress must have an old woman flying at her heels. In short, the whole air would be full of this kind of *gibier*, as the French call it.

Poets and writers of the time also echoed Addison's satire, wondering where the obsession with flying might lead. Would men come and go from one land to another, stealing what they fancied and flouting the laws? On the other hand, others felt there might be some advantages to wings, such as a means of travel which would do away with dirty and uncomfortable coach rides, and a wherewithal for the wealthy to leave their natural homes, colonize other planets, and—in a Biblical phrase—at last allow the meek to inherit the earth!

It is not surprising to find that the inventive Jonathan Swift was intrigued by the idea of flight, and created a huge flying 'island' for the third book of *Gulliver's Travels* (1726). In the intrepid captain's voyage to Laputa he sees a "vast opaque body between me and the sun, exactly circular, its diameter 7,837 yards, or about four miles and a half, and three hundred yards thick". This creation is inhabited by a race of people and propelled by a "lodestone of prodigious size". Obviously, because it has no wings, this is not the place to discuss Swift's unique creation, but the reader is simply directed to look at *Gulliver's Travels* again and ask himself whether he cannot see similarities between the 'island' and that controversial modern phenomenon, the flying saucer?

In 1727 there appeared another book which utilized the method of harnessing of birds to achieve flight—just as Godwin had done in his *Man in the Moone* nearly a hundred years before. This was *A Voyage to Cacklogallinia* by an author whose identity is known only by his pen-name 'Captain Samuel Brunt'. (Interestingly, for a time the book was variously attributed to Swift or Defoe because of its similarities to their work.)

The *Voyage* is, in essence, a satire on speculation, describing the financing of an expedition which would fly to the moon and there extract the gold which was said to lie in abundance in the mountains. Brunt's craft was a luxurious boat-shaped vehicle, carried by four large birds with four more in attendance as an escort. Although the craft does reach the moon, the gold project come to nothing because—like the South Sea Bubble speculation on which it was based—human greed proves its undoing.

The next work to interest us is a poem *Scribleriad* by Richard Owen Cambridge, published in 1751, which took up the theme of aerial warfare and the possibility of a contest for the skies. This theme increasingly interested scholars because of the problems they foresaw arising when man did finally take off into the heavens. The poem describes a contest between a German and a British youth:

> They spread their wings, and with a rising bound
> Swift at the words together quit the ground.

After a tough tussle, one of the Britisher's wings breaks and, defeated, he begins to tumble to the ground. But all is not lost, for

> Yet as he falls, so chance or fate decreed,
> His rival near him urg'd his winged speed,
> Nor unobserv'd (despair suggests a thought)
> Fast by the foot the heedless youth he caught,
> And drew the insulting victor to the ground:
> While rocks and woods with loud applause resound.

A graphic illustration of the cunning British youth grabbing his still-airborne opponent—who, incidentally, is wearing wings similar to those designed by the Frenchman Besnier—was published along with the poem and is reproduced in this book.

This same year there appeared a romance which for over one hundred years was as popular with readers as *Robinson Crusoe* and *Gulliver's Travels*, though today it is a forgotten item only treasured by collectors: *The Life and Adventures of Peter Wilkins* by Robert Paltock (1697–1767), an English lawyer and writer. This story of a race of winged men and women, the Gawreys and Glums, was a delight to ordinary readers and men of letters alike, and Robert Southey summed up the view of several generations when he wrote that he thought they were "the most beautiful creatures of imagination that ever were devised". Such was its success that it ran into many editions, was translated, pirated, imitated and turned into operas, dramas and even pantomimes. As so often happened at this period, the book contained a lengthy subtitle which summarizes the story far more successfully than any modern précis:

The Life and Adventures of Peter Wilkins
a Cornish Man

Relating particularly, His Shipwreck near the South Pole; his wonderful Passage thro' a subterraneous Cavern into a kind of New World; his meeting there with a Gawrey or flying Woman, whose Life he preserv'd, and afterwards married her; his extraordinary Conveyance to the Country, with the Laws, Customs and Manners of its Inhabitants, and the Author's remarkable Transactions among them. Taken from his own Mouth, in his Passage to England, from off Cape Horn in America, in the ship Hector. With an Introduction giving an account of the surprising Manner of his coming on board that Vessel, and his Death on his landing in Plymouth in the Year 1739. Illustrated with several Cuts, clearly and distinctly representing the Structure and Mechanism of the Wings of the Glums and Gawreys, and the manner in which they use either to swim or fly.

Paltock made full use of many of the theories and hopes of his lifetime relative to flying. He called his creatures' flying mechanism a "graundee" and gave it the additional capability of being able to be curled up into the shape of a boat and used for transport over water. He also provided a detailed description of the composition of these wings—basically long ribs or branches over which is stretched a "web of the softest and most pliable and springly membrane that can be imagined"—but his concept is most marvellously served by the illustrations which appeared in the book, two of which I have reproduced in these pages.

Another illustrated book of the same year was *The Adventures of John Daniel* by the Reverend Ralph Morris, in which a shipwrecked blacksmith from Royston in Hertfordshire invents a flying machine to escape from his island prison. The contrivance, or "Eagle" as Daniel calls it, is a large fixed wing, with smaller wings beneath, which are moved by a hand-pump operated by "the pilot". It proves such a success that Daniel crowns his freedom of the air by travelling to the moon. A drawing from the book is also reproduced in these pages.

It would have been a surprise indeed if the great Dr Samuel Johnson had not made some reference to the obsession with flight in his voluminous writing. In fact he twice dealt with the subject: the first occasion being in February 1752 when he wrote a letter to the *Rambler* magazine supposedly from a man who had injured himself in trying to fly; the second time, at greater length, occurs in his novel *Rasselas*, published in 1759.

A whole chapter entitled "A Dissertation on the Art of Flying" is included in the work in which Rasselas debates with "a man eminent for his knowledge of the mechanic powers" on the possibility of man-powered flight.

The mechanic tells him, "I have long been of the opinion that instead of the tardy conveyance of ships and chariots, man might use the swifter migration of wings, that the fields of air are open to knowledge, and that only ignorance and idleness crawl upon the ground". The secret of this, he says, is that "you will be necessarily upborne by the air if you can renew any impulse upon it, faster than the air can recede from the pressure".

Dr Johnson's expert has even settled on the style of his wings, as he tells Rasselas.

"I have considered the structure of all volant animals and find the folding continuity of the bat's wings most easily accommodated to the human form. Upon this model shall I begin my task tomorrow, and in a year expect to tour the air beyond the malice and pursuit of man."*

Before the close of the chapter, the mechanic tries his wings by leaping from a mountain top, but plunges straight into the lake below. It is only the quick intervention of Rasselas who is watching nearby that saves him from a watery grave.

Johnson's French contemporary Jean Jacques Rousseau similarly included the topic in *Le Nouveau Dedale* which may have been inspired by the somewhat ludicrous attempt of the Marquis de Bacqueville to fly in Paris in 1742 (we shall examine this attempt in the next chapter). Rousseau believed implicitly in the possibility of human flight and his work is basically a statement that it will be achieved soon by "a new Hero who will arrive to carry us all on wings into the heavens".

Two other significant novels—one English and the other French—appeared before the end of the eighteenth century and should be mentioned here: the extraordinary *Travels of Hildebrand Bowman Esquire* (1778) and Restif de la Bretonne's marvellous *La Découverte Australe par un Homme-Volant* published in 1781.

The anonymous author of *Hildebrand Bowman* begins his tale as a traditional shipwrecked-mariner story, but it rapidly becomes unique when his hero enters the land of Luxo-Volupto. Here he notices that some, but only some, of the people have wings, and inquires of his guide why this is. The man explains:

> About a century ago, when some became very loose, from the bad example of one of our Kings, a very surprising phenomenon made its appearance, the cause of which has never been accounted for in a natural way . . . This phenomenon is a pair of wings sprouting from every woman's shoulders, immediately after a failure in chastity; and from every man's who has seduced a young maiden, or married woman. As these are repeated, or according to the strength of their desires, the wings increase in size, till they become in full proportion to the body; and if the vice is left off from a sincere repentance, they gradually decrease till they entirely vanish.

* The idea of bats' wings serving as a model for winged flight is rarely found in the history of flight. One of the few other references to it in literature is in Benvenuto Cellini's autobiography where he discusses the idea with a mad Castellan. I have reproduced this extract as Appendix III.

Brown is also introduced to the "Alaeputas" or flying prostitutes, who have huge wings and evidently glory in their shame, and the aristocratic ladies who do not even bother to use their 'plumage' but are carried to and from their romantic assignations by "little cars to which are harnessed pigeons, pheasants or other birds". Despite the highly moral tone that the author tries to take towards these promiscuous people, freedom of the skies is seen in this instance to be won in a most pleasurable way!

Restif de la Bretonne's *La Découverte Australe par un Homme-Volant* has been described by experts as "The climax of the romantic conception of flight by artificial wings". Restif, who was born in 1734, is probably best known for his many licentious novels, yet in all his work he gives such a vividly truthful picture of eighteenth-centry French life that he is widely considered as an early proponent of literary realism.

The story of the *Homme-Volant* is similarly rooted in the social conditions of the time and concerns a young man of poor estate, Victorin, who is passionately in love with Christine, an arictocrat's daughter but secret Republican. For years he works to develop a pair of wings which will enable him to abduct the girl and carry her off to "a far-off land of liberty and equality for all". Having finally perfected his equipment, he sweeps down on the girl as she walks to church one Sunday morning and carries her off over the mountains. In their new land the couple find true happiness, raise a family, and even develop a second set of wings so that both can fly all over the world.

Another enthusiast of Restif de la Bretonne's work is Charles Gibbs-Smith, who wrote recently:

Apart from the popularity of this romance, the illustrations may well have inspired many a young man's interest in the air. Technically, the flying equipment is worth noting. The special flying-suit, to which the wings are fastened, has attachments for supply baskets, and a sling for the lady to sit in. But most interesting is the parachute above his head, shown shut in the abduction scene, which is the first representation of a parachute in modern history. This may even have led Blanchard towards his experiments.

Important though this work is, there was in fact a study published slightly earlier by another Frenchman which also brought to a finale the literary aspirations on the possibility of flight in the seventeenth and eighteenth centuries. The work was *Le Philosophie sans Prétention ou l'Homme Rare* by the French scientist and chemist Louis-Guillaume de la Follie, which appeared in 1775. The book was a mixture of contemporary science and fantasy, but contained the description of a flying chariot powered by *electricity*—the first time such a proposal had been made.

La Follie describes how this machine will enable man to fly wherever he chooses without the danger inherent in wings or other methods. The chariot, with its wheels, globes of glass, springs and wires—not forgetting a platform for the aeronauts—is demonstrated to a disbelieving audience and goes through a most alarming series of dives and swift climbs before shooting off towards the planets. In its concept and description the author had successfully embodied all the discoveries about the principles of flight from the previous century and before.

Just as Restif's work had marked the climax of the *romantic* conception of flight, so La Follie's marks the *scientific* climax. There was practically nothing left for human speculation in this area: reality had to follow and indeed, in 1783, after all those centuries of dreams and plans, man finally took to the air when the brothers Montgolfier sailed slowly up into the heavens in their balloon.

Marjorie Hope Nicolson has described this moment superbly:

Yet, as the balloons of the Montgolfiers, Lunardi, Charles, Blanchard and others symbolize a beginning, so they mark the end of a long period of trial and error, of conjecture, of occasional happy guesses. They mark the end, too, of a peculiar form of literature. The 'Cosmic Voyage' will go on, but after the invention of the balloon it suffers a change into something, I think, less rich and strange. Science has conquered fancy. Man, having learned the laws of nature, has mastered nature and harnessed her forces to his will.

This is not the end of the dream of winged—or man-powered—flight, however; true, the exploits of birdmen which went on during the literary period we have just covered are in the main eccentric and amusing. But, as we shall see, man goes resolutely on wrestling with his ageless desire, and, in attempting to succeed, varies his approach by diversification into gliding and its later off-shoots.

But first we have a century and more of bizarre but factual exploits to look at before the Montgolfier balloon goes up. . . .

The dream of flight has been a constant theme in literature: this illustration accompanied Martin Tupper's essay "A Flight Upon Flying" (1850)

[8]

Eccentric Wings and the Ascent of the Balloon

As has been observed so often in history, art was merely imitating nature when the numerous works of fantasy fiction appeared in the eighteenth century. Although, as I have already noted, there was little practical achievement during this epoch, there was a goodly number of eccentric attempts at flight with wings or in flying machines which are worthy of study. Several critics have already pointed out the importance that 'aerial fiction' played in stimulating public interest, and perhaps the bizarre nature of so many of the romances can be held responsible for some of the equally strange human endeavours!

A slightly earlier event which we should not pass over is the proposal and design for a flying machine in 1670 by the Italian philosopher and scientist, Francesco Lana. The importance of his idea is in the use of four globes made of thin copper to carry aloft a passenger 'chariot', and of sails and oars to propel and direct it. Lana, of course, knew nothing of the specific lightness of heated air and of hydrogen gas—these discoveries were not to be made until the later part of the eighteenth century—but he believed that if all the air was extracted from his globes, they would naturally rise. He equated the air with water, thinking "it has weight owing to the vapours and halations which ascend from the earth and seas" and therefore designed his 'chariot' with the means to rise and be propelled through it. His machine never flew, naturally enough, for even if the globes had been made airless, they would have collapsed under the atmospheric pressure; the wind, too, would have carried the craft whichever way it blew, regardless of the 'steering' devices. Nonetheless, his invention established the 'lighter-than-air' principle and it only remains a surprise that so much time was to elapse before anyone thought of taking his idea further.

The eighteenth century was nine years old before the next significant development in man's pursuit of flight occurred—the invention of a fantastic airship by a theologian and priest, Father Laurenco de Gusmao. Gusmao was born in Santos, Brazil, in 1686, but lived most of his life in Portugal. He was involved in speculation about flight from his student days, and in 1709 applied to the King of Portugal, Juan V, for a patent for the flying machine he had designed.

Although there is much controversy surrounding this man, it is believed that he built a miniature version of his "Passarola" (Great Bird), as he called the machine, and made it fly briefly before the King in June 1709. The King was so amazed that he granted Gusmao honour and finance to continue his work. A full-size model was later prepared, but as one can judge from the illustration of it which survives—undoubtedly fantasized very considerably—it never left the ground. This picture has certainly contributed to the ridicule that many people have heaped upon Gusmao—saying he was a charlatan and had merely included all the known ideas for lifting and flying in one unlikely contrivance to gain royal approval. Recent commentators, however, re-examining the inventor's papers, believe his actual design was rather more workable, and have advanced the claim that he was the first pioneer of practical aeronautics in Europe.

After the failure of his full-size "Passarola", Gusmao is believed to have developed a new version with fixed wings, and reliable evidence suggests that this actually flew from the walls of a castle in Lisbon late in 1709. "If this glider did fly," John W. R. Taylor has written, "it was the first aeroplane in history. Nor did it mark the end of Gusmao's achievements, for it is almost certain that he demonstrated a model hot-air 'balloon' before the King of Portugal in that same year, preceding by seventy-four years the Montgolfier brothers, who are usually credited with inventing the balloon."

This balloon, according to a contemporary report, "consisted of a small bark in the form of a trough which was covered with a cloth of canvas". Gusmao demonstrated it before King

Juan in the Salla das Embaixadas and "with various spirits, quintessences and other ingredients he put a light beneath it, and let the said bark fly before His Majesty and many other persons". Unfortunately the report goes on, as the contrivance rose into the air, it struck against some curtains in the hall and set them on fire, and then tumbled to the ground itself, also dissolving into flames. The King, though, "was good enough not to take ill", the account concludes.

After this event, Gusmao's life is shrouded in mystery and there is no record that he repeated any of his experiments. Charles Gibbs-Smith, who believes this Portuguese ecclesiastic may be an even more important figure in the history of aviation than has been heretofore suspected, says of Gusmao's last years until his death in 1724, "There was said to have been talk of sorcery and the Inquisition, but no evidence exists to show he was persecuted. He seems, however, to have left mysteriously for Spain some years later."

A far less mysterious figure who contributed to our history at this time was the Swedish writer, mathematician and scientist Emmanuel Swedenborg (1688–1772). Swedenborg, with his intense interest in mysticism and religion, considered flight from both a technical and a symbolic viewpoint and was undoubtedly an avid reader of the 'cosmic voyages' published during his lifetime. He also invented a flying machine which—though it was never built—has obviously been the subject of much deliberation.

The contrivance had certain similarities to the "Passarola" and consisted of a boat built of cork, a widely stretched sail parallel to this and forming a hollow, and two wings to be worked up and down by a spiral spring. "These wings," Swedenborg wrote in 1714, "should be in the shape of birds' wings, or the sails of a windmill, or some such shape, and should be tilted obliquely upwards, and made so as to collapse on the upward stroke and expand on the downward." He added, as a footnote, "The wings would perhaps have greater force, so as to increase the resistance and make the flight easier, if a hood or shield were placed over them, as is the case with certain insects."

It was perhaps the very unlikeliness of the machines of Lana and Gusmao—not forgetting that of Swedenborg—which failed to promote further study, and for the next half-century we find a continuing string of eccentric birdmen holding the stage. These men were obviously not deterred by previous failure, nor the recent argument by Giovanni Borelli that man's own strength unaided would never lift him into the skies. Their rewards were—of course—failure, lampooning in the press, burlesque on the stage, and the derision of the public throughout Europe.

The most notable of these escapades was surely that of an eccentric French nobleman, the Marquis de Bacqueville, who caught the aeronautical 'bug' in middle age and actually decided to try and fly himself when he was 62 years old!

The Marquis, a man of extravagant tastes and wild opinions, is believed to have been inspired to make his attempt by that of Besnier in 1678. For this purpose he had constructed wings, or paddles, to be fitted on his arms and legs. It was his intention, he said, to fly from his home in Paris on the Quai des Théatins (today the Quai Voltaire) across the Seine to the other bank.

Eccentric though the old man undoubtedly was, he did not trust implicitly in his wings and decided that it would be best if one of his servants tried them out first. The man he selected to be his guinea-pig, says a later account, was his *valet de chambre*. The luckless servant, knowing that he risked dismissal for refusing, had a sudden happy flash of inspiration as he hesitated to reply. He would claim precedence as his excuse.

"Monsieur le Marquis," he said respectfully, "a valet cannot possibly precede his master. It is out of the question."

The dumfounded Marquis had, of course, no answer, and aware of the vast crowd that had now assembled on both banks of the Seine to watch the attempt, he had to strap the wings on himself. Climbing onto a top-floor window-ledge, he paused for a moment and then took a mighty leap. Furiously he flapped his arms and legs up and down, but to no avail. He swept down, just missing the pavement, and falling onto old clothes in a washerwoman's boat which had pulled up alongside the *quai* to watch him. This proved the saving of the old gentleman, for he sustained only a broken leg.

Monsieur le Marquis appears not to have made any more attempts at flight, but his endeavour was widely publicized and excited much comment. Modern experts believe that the illustration of the Frenchman's attempt—shown elsewhere—

The Wright brothers' first glider – the prototype for their aircraft which finally lifted man into the heavens for sustained and controlled flight under engine-power

L'Homme volant.

Gravure sur bois pour un roman du *Magasin des Demoiselles* [con]sacré à la vieille légende des hommes volants aperçus dans [la] nuit, à la clarté de la lune, fendant l'espace à travers monts et [va]ux et planant au-dessus des villes.

Quand les hommes seront oiseaux, et quand les oiseaux seront hommes.

(*Pasquino*, de Turin, 1909.)

Une image de l'avenir pouvant prendre place parmi les curieuses estampes qu'on appelait autrefois *le monde renversé*.

— Vois comme il vole vers le ciel, le *Ibis sacra* Gabriel!

(*Pasquino*, de Turin, 19 septembre 1909.)

Amusante caricature sur d'Annunzio. — L'ibis sacré, ou le *deux fois saint* Gabriel.

— Tiens! vous vous livrez à l'aéronautique?
— Que voulez-vous? N'est-ce pas l'unique moyen possible de locomotion, à Milan.

(*Illustrazione Italiana*.)

Appareil protecteur co[ntre] tre la chute des homm[es] volants.

Brevèté et patenté p[ar] le *Kiderik* (mai 1909).

A selection of 'birdman' cartoons from early twentieth-century European publications

(*above*) Another aerial performer in the tradition of Vincent de Groof; he was known simply as "The Bat" and seems to have avoided the fate of his predecessor (from the *Illustrated Police News*)

(*below*) Another birdman from Italy, who apparently made several successful flights over Florence and Rome

Lilienthal's British pupil, Percy Pilcher, in "The Hawk"; he was killed while flying this glider in 1898

A model of one of the man-powered aircraft built by the Japanese inventor Chuchachi Ninimiya at the turn of the century

Three old photographs
showing lessons taking
place at the flying
school in Lille, France

(*above*) An American birdman experimenting with aluminium wings. No record exists as to his success or otherwise. (*below*) The American pioneer, Major R. Franklin-Moore of Washington, with his "Flying Fox Wings"

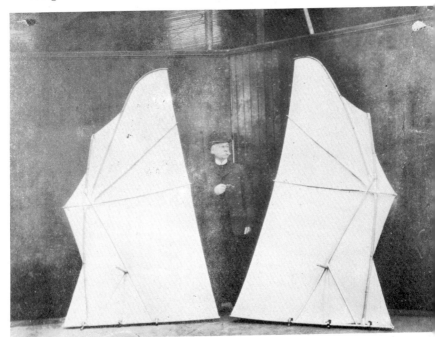

An attempt to get airborne with a bicycle and a rigid glider wing in a Paris park in the early 1900s

The aeroplane bicycle of the Count de Guiseux, with which he is said to have achieved short hops along the ground

"Rickman's Flying Machine" was based on the principle that two cyclists should succeed where one had failed

The tragic death of the German birdman Gross-Lichterfeld in Berlin, as recorded by a contemporary artist (1896)

A satirical cartoon on the use of winged men in warfare

(*left*) The Haessler-Villinger pedal-driven aircraft built in the 1930s, for which moderately successful flights were claimed. (*below*) The hand-propelled aeroplane developed by Gaston Mourlaque of Levallois-Perret in France, which he claims has flown. The plane can also operate on a motor

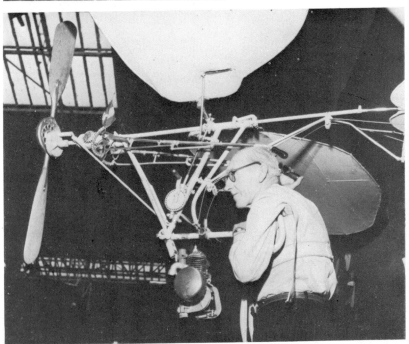

The Pedalcopter designed by American Naval Attorney Charles Paul and flown successfully at Lakehurst, New Jersey. It weighs 140 pounds and is suspended below a 24-foot-diameter balloon. The pilot uses his feet to drive the helicopter blades which aid in raising and steering the Pedalcopter

Flight Lieutenant
John Potter at the
controls of "Puffin"
– in which he
achieved the world
man-powered flight
record of 1,171
yards in 1972.
(*below*) A detailed
drawing of
"Puffin's" cockpit
by Dick Ellis

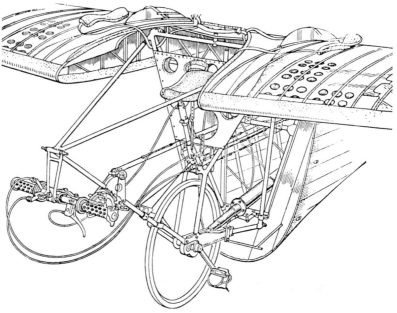

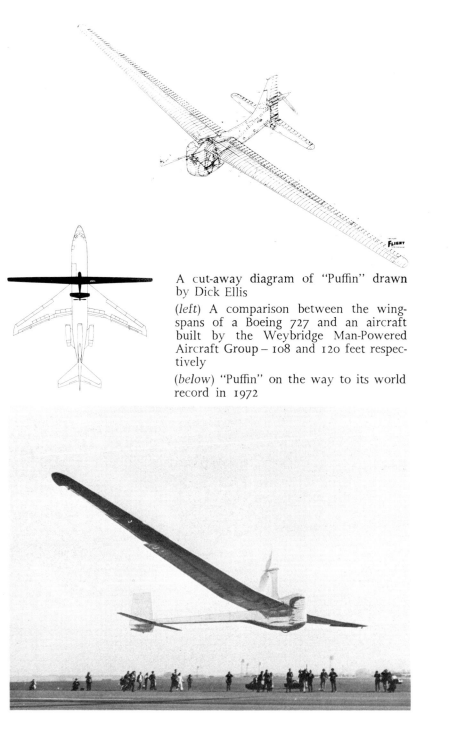

A cut-away diagram of "Puffin" drawn by Dick Ellis

(*left*) A comparison between the wing-spans of a Boeing 727 and an aircraft built by the Weybridge Man-Powered Aircraft Group – 108 and 120 feet respectively

(*below*) "Puffin" on the way to its world record in 1972

(*above*) Pedalling into the sky: the successful "Skycycle" designed by the Austrian Josef Malliga, in which he has made numerous man-powered flights. (*below*) The ornithopter developed by London sculptor Emile Hartman, costing £3,000. The feathered wings have a span of 36 feet, but have so far proved too fragile to lift the machine off the ground

The cycle-biplane built for £20 by Leslie Smith, senior briefing officer of the Aeronautical Information Service at Heathrow Airport. Even with one of Heathrow's runways to use for launching, Smith was unable to get his 130-pound machine off the ground

Enea Bossi, the Italian immigrant who, some experts believe, was the first birdman to pedal himself into the air – in New York in 1937

(*above*) An Italian entrant for the Kremer Prize, Umberto Carnevali, known to his friends as the "Fly Man", with the craft he hopes to fly at Urbe Airport, near Rome, where he works. (*left*) Chris Lovell of the Surrey Gliding Club at the controls of the Weybridge Man-Powered Aircraft Group's plane which he managed to pedal for about 50 yards at a height of 3 feet in 1971

does not accurately convey his equipment, and as he did not fall directly down from the window-ledge, he may well have used a form of rigid glider wing.

The Italians were, naturally enough, still providing intrepid birdmen from their ranks, and there are numerous stories of Tito Burattini having made several attempts in his homeland—all without success, but with little personal damage. Burattini's method of flight was said to take the form of a single-hinged wing strapped across the shoulder blades.

When he ventured further afield, no doubt hoping to enrich himself by his daring, Burattini is reported to have twice made short flights before King Wladyslaw of Poland and his court. The accounts are confusing in that some insist that the Italian attempted flight under his own power, while others say he built a machine aided by sails. In the event, we can only really be sure of Burattini's bravery.

Also in eastern Europe, we come across stories at this time of another 'flying monk', one Brother Cyprian, who is said to have devoted himself equally to "prayer and flying as one of God's angels". The monk allegedly built himself wings of cloth stretched across a fixed framework, and using this equipment "glided down from the peak of a mountain in Eastern Europe". The brother's flight—or flights—have been variously dated from 1750 to 1780.

There are also brief reports from this same period of a Bohemian inventor named Fucik who made himself wings of wood, feathers, paper and springs, and enjoyed several trips without damage to himself. Again the authenticity of the success must be questioned, though the attempts are in all probability true.

Similar mystery surrounds the story of an Englishman named John Childs, who is said to have tried to fly with home-made wings in the 1750s. There are few details of his equipment, save that the wings were made of a specially treated fabric, and Childs himself wore a one-piece suit of leather which was fastened with thongs and cord. He is also credited with having attempted another flight from a tower in Boston, America—and if this was the case he probably qualifies as one of the very earliest American birdmen. However, modern commentators believe that the whole story is untrue and was based on a misinterpretation of early records.

G

Another Englishman, named Cadman, who met an unhappy end while trying to fly at this time, is commemorated with the following lines which appear on his tombstone in St Mary's Church, Shrewsbury. They are probably far more evocative than any modern retelling of the story could be:

> Let this small monument record the name,
> Of Cadman, and to future times proclaim,
> How, by an attempt to fly from this high spire,
> Across the widening stream, he did acquire,
> His fatal end. 'Twas not for want of skill,
> Or courage to perform the task, he fell;
> No, no; a faulty cord being drawn too tight,
> Hurried his soul on high to take her flight,
> Which bid the body here goodnight.
>
> Aged 28.

February 2nd 1739.

In 1764, a German named Melchoir Bauer drew up plans for a flying machine not unlike that specified by Swedenborg. It consisted of a small carriage fixed by braces to a large wing with flaps which was made to move up and down by a series of rockers worked by the aeronaut. The wing worked in two sections: when one side was rising with its flaps in an open position, the other side was falling with its flaps closed—thus the machine achieved a rearward thrust. Although recently new documents on Bauer and his invention have been discovered in the Staatsarchiv at Greiz, it has not yet proved possible to ascertain whether his contrivance was ever actually built and tested.

Another machine in the same mould which was built and tested was the brainchild of the ecclesiast Canon Desforges of the Collegiate Church of Saint Croix d'Etampes in France. This *voiture volante* consisted of a wickerwork basket, manually operated wings and a huge fabric canopy to help support it in the air and also apparently, to help guard it from crashing. In 1772, the canon announced that he would demonstrate his invention by flying "on wings" to Paris, and "multitudes of the curious flocked to Etampes", says a contemporary report.

The account goes on, "The *abbé*'s machine was a sort of gondola, seven feet long and about two feet deep. Gondola, conductor and baggage weighed in all 213 pounds. The pious man believed that he had provided against everything. Neither tempest nor rain should mar his flight, and there was no chance of his being upset; whilst the machine, he had decided, was to go at the rate of thirty leagues (sixty miles) an hour."

At the appointed hour, the canon appeared and entered his machine to muffled cheers and laughter. He sat down and began to work the wings with ever-increasing rapidity. "But," said an eye-witness later, "the more he worked, the more his machine cleaved to the earth, as if it were part and parcel of it."

Some chroniclers report that the humiliated man had a second try at making his craft fly by having it launched from the Tour de Guinette, the ruins of which can still be seen near Etampes Station, but again the wings beat vainly against the air and it crashed straight to the ground. The machine was completely smashed and the canon broke several bones.

A decade later, in 1781, another notable pioneer who is virtually forgotten today emerged—Carl Friedrich Meerwin, the architect to the German Prince of Baden. He designed and built what has been called a glided-ornithopter. This device, which Meerwin described in his pamphlet *L'Art de voler à la Manière des Oiseaux* (published in 1784) consisted of two large wings which looked pear-shaped in repose.

Meerwin had calculated that he needed 126 square feet of wing surface to support himself, and hanging beneath this he caused the wings to beat up and down by a mechanism which is not specified. Experts believe that he may well have made one or two short glides, but the absence of a tail or other auxiliary surfaces prevented any kind of sustained flight.

This same year, in France, Jean Pierre Blanchard, who later became famed as the first 'professional' balloonist, constructed and experimented with a *vaisseau volant* which was basically a boat enclosed by a tent-like structure through which numerous 'paddles' projected. The pilot used these to row the 'flying ship' through the air.

According to some reports, Blanchard actually managed to sustain himself in the air for a few moments in this bizarre creation. Certainly it was on display in a hotel garden in Paris during 1782 and attracted enormous crowds. However, immediately after the success of the Mongolfier brothers, Blanchard worked on a method of harnessing his ship to the balloon, and in March 1784 brought his scheme to fruition when the flying machine was lifted majestically into the air beneath a balloon from the Champ de Mars.

From the experience, Blanchard quickly learned that his oars were of no use in aerial navigation, and thereafter switched his attention wholly to balloon flights. During the closing years of the century he was the most popular balloonist in France, and was also responsible for introducing the art of ballooning to the American people—though he had to guard carefully against the actions of hooligans and the superstitious who constantly wanted to destroy his balloons.

Activities such as those of Blanchard stimulated experiment throughout France and it is no surprise to learn of a certain A. J. Renaux who designed an ornithopter in which the pilot stood in a wooden framework and moved a series of wings by wooden levers; and of a Monsieur Aries who flew or glided a considerable distance before numerous witnesses at Avignon in July 1784.

In 1784, also, another French inventor became one of the first men to realize that an engine would be necessary for heavier-than-air flying. He was a man named Gérard who proposed a rocket-shaped machine with huge wings and a rudder. What made his plan unique was his "gunpowder motor" to flap the wings, with the "escaping gases, like a rocket" driving the machine forward. The machine, which was never built, was also to have a specially sprung landing device.

However, for the moment, the eyes and attention of all those involved in aeronautics in any way—and the general public for that matter—were concentrated on something quite different. For, just a year before, on 19th September 1783, the Montgolfier brothers, Joseph and Étienne, had been responsible for one of the great moments in aviation history: they had actually achieved flight in a hot-air balloon.

Even before the time of the Montgolfiers, the principles of aerostation had begun to be recognized, though nothing had been done to act upon them. In 1766, the English chemist Henry Cavendish, realized and defined the true properties of hydrogen, which he called "inflammable gas". Almost immediately, Dr Joseph Black, the Professor of Anatomy and Chemistry at Glasgow University, concluded that a thin glass or bladder filled with this gas would naturally rise, and demonstrated this to his students. Black considered the experiment purely one of amusement and did not for a moment consider developing a container large enough to raise a man.

A third man, Tiberius Cavallo, almost gave birth to the balloon age when he published his *History and Practice of Aerostation* in 1785. Taking the idea of Professor Black's "bladders of gas", he filled soap bubbles with this light air and saw how they rose in the air. However, when he tried to extend this work further by making a container of paper, he found the material was porous and most of the gas escaped before it could rise. Short of patience, he abandoned the experiment— and left it to the Montgolfiers to reap the honour which was so nearly his.

Joseph and Étienne, who had a papermaking business near Lyons, are said to have received their inspiration from watching the little pieces of burning paper spiralling up the chimney from their fire. Although they did not appreciate what was really happening, they decided that if this hot, rising air could be trapped, it would cause any object to rise. Following experiments with a small silk bag held over an open fire, they progressed to a huge spherical balloon filled from a special fire of wool and straw, and found that resulting from centuries of endeavour they had inadvertently discovered the secret of flight. Within weeks they were national heroes, and scientists and aeronautical experts everywhere began to work on perfecting their discovery. Man could now fly!

As the development of ballooning is a complex story and plays little further part in our history of man-powered flight, the reader seeking further information is directed to the several histories of ballooning which have been published, including this author's *The Dream Machines* (New English Library, 1972) a lavishly illustrated study with contemporary reports and accounts by leading experts.

[9]

The Realization of Flight

The evolution of the balloon, and the rapid development of both the hot-air and the hydrogen varieties, did not deter the birdmen and 'flappers'. As before when some giant stride had been made in aeronautics, there were still those who persisted in their belief that man could fly under his own power, if only the right technique and equipment could be devised. As we turn into the eighteenth century, we find several such intrepid experimenters, one notable old gentleman taking off with wings at the age of 72!

This extraordinary man was a French general, Resnier de Goué, who had been experimenting with wings both before and after the Montgolfier's success, but probably not making his first actual attempt until as late as 1788. The well-known illustration of de Goué's wings and harness was made in 1801, when he made a flight over the River Charente, and shows his equipment quite clearly. The birdman dived off the picturesque ramparts of the city of Angoulême and, flapping furiously, gained several yards before splashing into the water. He was, as I said earlier, 72 years old at the time! (Some reports claim that de Goué attempted another flight a little later, this time over land. He is said to have fallen heavily, broken a leg, and although deterred from any further attempts himself, remained convinced of the possibility of man-powered flight until his death.)

An equally notorious character was a Swiss clockmaker named Jacob Degen who utilized the discovery of the balloon to gain a long-standing reputation that he could fly unaided. Degen (1756–1846), who lived and worked in Vienna, designed his *Flugmaschine* (shown opposite) along ornithopter principles. The contrivance had 130 square feet of wing area which was worked by the aeronaut, opening on the upstroke and closing on the down. To test its power, Degen in 1809 attached the machine to a large hydrogen balloon and found that this would take him up into the skies.

Soon the clockmaker had earned a reputation in the news-papers—which he did nothing to dispute—that he could fly unaided, and very few of the surviving illustrations of him show his craft supported by a balloon. This deception worked against Degen in October 1812, however, when he put on a

Degen being set upon by an angry crowd in Paris in 1812

much-heralded display in Paris and—failing to satisfy the crowd—was branded as a "miserable charlatan" and was attacked and injured by a group of incensed bystanders.

Degen was undoubtedly a serious experimenter, though, and he can claim to have provided the inspiration for the York-shireman Sir George Cayley, who propounded the first prac-ticable powered aeroplane in 1809. This "most powerful genius in the history of aviation", according to the historian Charles Dollfus, made the vital step of proposing a system of thrust for an aeroplane *as well as* the system of lift. His story and experiments are now a part of the opening chapter of the aircraft *per se*, and with it we leave the main flow of aeronautical history to follow our own tributory story.

Degen was also imitated by a German tailor named Albrecht Berblinger who was taken in by the illustrations of the Swiss flying unaided. With a machine of a similar design—but unsupported by a balloon—he jumped off some high scaffolding on the banks of the River Danube at Ulm in 1811 and plunged straight into the water, "much to the malicious glee of the assembled crowd", says a report. Fortunately, he was quickly rescued and found to be unhurt.

Even years later, Degen's alleged flights were said still to be inspiring others, as the *London Journal* somewhat mysteriously reports in its issue of 19th December 1846: "The *Rhine Gazette* publishes a letter from Dr Hecke of Brussels, in which he asserts that he had discovered the means of aerial travelling at any height that he pleases. He states that he has solicited the appointment of an official committee to examine his discovery, as he is already prepared to show that he has the means of supporting a carriage in the air without any *point d'appui*." A look at the *Rhine Gazette* reveals an illustration of the good Dr Hecke's craft, which is identical to Degen's in almost every respect—but no balloon!

The next significant figure in man-powered flight was an English portrait painter and spare-time inventor, Thomas Walker, who in 1810 published a thesis in which he presented his own design for an ornithopter. The work was called *A*

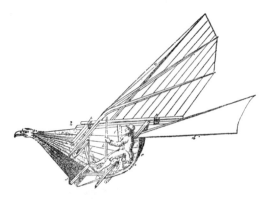

Thomas Walker's ornithopter

Treatise on the Art of Flying by Mechanical Means and Walker's craft—as our illustration shows—was manipulated by both the hands and feet. Although this invention was hopelessly impractical, Walker's later idea for a tandem fixed-wing monoplane (1831) was ultimately to influence Blériot, and he was among the first to propose that aircraft might be used for exploration and carrying the mail.

Another French eccentric, the Count Adolphe de Lambertye, proposed a man-powered ornithopter in 1818 with enormous wings which would have required the strength of a Samson to move them, let alone generate any speed. His extraordinary plan, which was apparently never built, is perhaps only worth remembering because he also suggested that a form of helicopter should be devised to take passengers from the ground to their aerial transporter. (The first successful helicopter device had already been devised and tested by this time—the invention of two Frenchmen, Launcy and Bienvenu, in 1784. They had finally brought to fruition the great Leonardo's idea of two hundred years earlier.)

Ten years later, an English carpenter, David Meyer, built a large man-powered helicopter which, though it never left the ground, performed in a manner which its inventor described as "very flattering, though not perfectly successful".

The Frenchman L. C. Letur also had reason to be pleased with his strange machine, a mixture of parachute-cum-glider, which he unveiled in 1853. This was pulled into the air by a balloon and then released to glide down, and, indeed, Letur made several successful and highly publicized descents. In July 1854, however, the machine became entangled in some trees during a descent over Paris and he was killed. The same fate also awaited a contemporary, Bréant, whose enormous wings were worked to and fro by cords fastened to his arms and legs.

One of the earliest photographs in aeronautical history is of a huge glider with a wingspan of 23 feet built to resemble an albatross by the French sea-captain and inventor, J. M. Le Bris in 1857. Le Bris had found his inspiration while watching these birds on his many sea voyages, and in the years between 1857 and 1868 made several attempts at Trefeuntec (when the photograph was taken). To launch his 'bird' he placed it on a farm cart which was galloped downhill, and at the moment of greatest speed he would release the restraining ropes. He is said to have achieved one short glide, but mostly he met with failure, and indeed had to abandon his project when he broke a leg in a bad crash. Nonetheless he was one of the earliest pioneers in practical flying.

During this same period an Englishman, F. H. Wenham, had been making tests with a multiplane glider, that is, one with five wings. He had implemented Sir George Cayley's proposal for cambered wings, and though he met with little actual success, he demonstrated quite clearly that such wings obtained most of their lift from the front portion. Wenham published his findings in the first report of the Royal Aeronautical Society of Great Britain in 1866, and they were both widely read and influential on later experimentors.

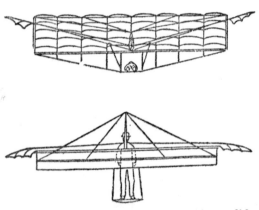

F. H. Wenham's design for a multiplane glider

A wealthy French industrialist who had nursed a life-long fascination with flight decided to do something concrete to advance its progress in the 1860s. The man, J. J. Boucart, who had himself designed an ornithopter with two pairs of feathered wings which unfortunately did not live up to any of his high expectations, offered two prizes for those who succeeded where he had failed. In doing so he initiated the first of many offers with a financial inducement which have attracted man-powered enthusiasts to this very day.

Boucart offered a reward of 5,000 francs for the first flight of twenty minutes, and a second prize of 2,000 francs for a duration of five minutes at no less than three metres above the ground. Though there were several who tried, the philanthropist eventually died with his offer unclaimed.

Two fellow countrymen, Struve and Telescheff, who thought they had found the answer by building an ornithopter with five pairs of wings—believing that these would give the machine the stability which single-winged contrivances lacked —were sadly disappointed when they underwent trials in 1864. So was a man named Claudel who built an extraordinary machine which consisted of a combination of fixed wings and longitudinally rotating surfaces which were to serve as propellers.

A man who did achieve some moderate success in 1868 was an Englishman named Charles Spencer who built a machine which had two fixed wings with an area of 110 square feet and a long, pointed tail. Its novelty was two 'flappers' of approximately 15 square feet, which were attached to the end of the wings and activated by man-power. Spencer is said to have flown this craft on several occasions for small distances, and even gone on to develop a delta-wing successor. However, whether failure to achieve complete success or just decreasing interest, caused him to go on to other things, the records do not make clear.

Experts are agreed, however, that the most outstanding man of the 1860s was a French Count, Ferdinand Philipe d'Esterno, who in 1864 published an important work, *Du Vol des Oiseaux*. M. J. B. Davy writes:

> This book was of great importance, as it was the first to draw attention to the soaring—as opposed to gliding—flight of birds. D'Esterno might almost be said to have 'discovered' soaring and wrote, "in soaring flight, a man can handle an apparatus carrying 10 tons, just as well as one carrying only his own weight." Incidentally, d'Esterno's passages on the sliding seat for the pilot, to alter the machine's centre of gravity, may well have influenced Lilienthal in his choice of the hang-glider type of machine, in which the pilot hangs in the machine by his arms and swings his hips and legs in any direction he desires.

As a result of his research, d'Esterno designed and patented the first machine for soaring—it included wings whose angles could be changed—but never actually built a prototype.

At this point in our history, we find that more and more of the new contrivances endeavouring to fly included some form of motive form, be it a gas engine (Lenoir had invented this in 1860), steam-power, twisted rubber or even bullets!* The internal combustion engine was not, of course, to open up vast new possibilities until the German N. A. Otto produced his four-stroke engine in 1876. There were, though, those who still sought man-powered flight, and it has been claimed that the sudden increase of numbers in the face of all the evidence was due to the publication in 1873 of a book called *La Machine Animale* by Professor Étienne Marey.

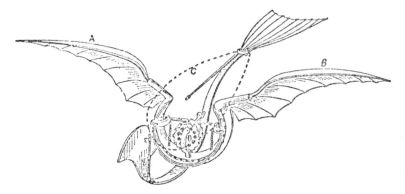

Gustave Trouvé's ornithopter driven by blank revolver cartridges!

The book was remarkable in that it contained a sequence of photographs of a bird flying and brought into close focus many of the problems of flight. Marey also photographed the flow of wind over bodies of various shapes by using smoke in a wind tunnel. According to Charles Gibbs-Smith, this book was a source of inspiration to the Wright brothers, but "to its less mature readers, it unhappily inspired further ideas of strange construction". A few general examples from various quarters will suffice to represent what was happening.

* There was perhaps no more bizarre creation than the model made in 1870 by the Frenchman Gustave Trouvé which some authorities believe actually flew. This creation—see illustration—was driven by blank revolver cartridges which were fired automatically into a tube and thus caused the wings to beat down; springs then returned them in time for the next firing of cartridges. It was claimed that after being launched in mid-air, the weird craft could fly for approximately 200 feet. Perhaps mercifully, Trouvé never built a full-size version!

An unlikely interpretation was that of W. P. Quimby, one of the earliest American birdmen, who lived in Wilmington, Ohio. Quimby was convinced that man was "a species of featherless bird", and returned to the idea of harnessing wings to the strongest muscles of the body. His design—complete with tail, printed elsewhere—was included in several American newspapers in 1874, and although one editor advised any readers who might try to emulate Mr Quimby to do so from a low take-off point, added optimistically, "However, we may say that the principle of calling into play the strong muscles of the thighs to aid the arms in the movement of the wings is taking advantage of the greatest power the human body can exert, and in this the device is an improvement upon some other attempts."

Another American, John Holmes of Oak Valley, Kansas, proposed a more likely-looking contrivance with his "Improved Airship", the plans of which were made public in the last quarter of the century. With the illustration reproduced in this book went the following description by Holmes:

> The horizontal frame of the machine is suspended by hanger bars or rods from an aerofoil which is a frame covered by a silken fabric. Towards its rear there is attached to the side bars of the horizontal frame a canvas forming a support on which the aeronaut will lie, so that his hands may conveniently reach two transverse cranked shafts by working one of which he can rotate a propeller wheel at the front. At the rear is a rudder sail which can be guided by the feet.

It was claimed that once the craft was launched into the air, its surfaces could be locked to utilize the currents of the wind to the best advantage. Although ridiculous in most aspects, there are here more of the glimmers of invention which will eventually lead to the pedal-power machines of the twentieth century.

The same can also be said of the Frenchman A. Goupil's "aerial velocipede" which was unveiled at this time. This craft, made of wood covered with silk, weighed only 220 pounds. Reporting on it, the *Chronique Industrielle* said:

> The man, in order to obtain speed, acts at one and the same time, through the pedals (marked a) and the connecting rods (b) upon a wheel that moves over the ground, and through jointed arms (c) upon the helix (e); and he likewise acts upon the

rudder (f) and the tail lever by means of cords. As the apparatus obtains velocity its weight diminishes on account of the increase of the vertical reaction of the current, and, finally, it ought to ascend and maintain itself aloft solely through the motion of the helix combined with the sustaining action of the wings and regulating and directing action of the rudder. Equilibrium must be maintained through the displacement of the man's centre of gravity.

The publication was not able to report whether the machine had ever left the ground, but added optimistically,

> However, if it is allowable to smile innocently at its claims, it is perhaps less allowable to have doubts. The rules of mechanics do not contradict the assertion that it will one day be possible for man to rise and direct himself in the air when the latter is undisturbed by storms. When aluminium and still lighter and more powerful motors shall intervene, the solution of the problem will not have to be long awaited.

A contemporary of Goupil, one Pompeien Piraud, built a bat-shaped ornithopter which was intended to be launched from a balloon with the appropriate name of *L'Espérance*, but there is no record of any such attempts. Another Frenchman, Pierre Dandrieux, launched his ornithopter in 1872. Dandrieux had become impressed by recent reports that the tips of birds' wings acted like airscrews, and consequently designed his contrivances to imitate these movements. The pilot sat between two wings and worked a series of levers that turned screw-like propellers. Unfortunately, for all his study and hard work, Dandrieux only achieved some jerky hops across the ground.

1874 saw the most interesting of all these contrivances, an ornithopter that was part 'flapper' and part parachute, designed and built by a Belgian named Vincent de Groof. De Groof, who was a shoemaker by profession, had dreamed and read about flight since his boyhood, and by the late 1860s had experimented with enough models to try constructing his own machine. He planned for his contrivance—shown elsewhere— to be pulled up into the heavens by a balloon and then released. According to a contemporary report, "he intended to emulate the flight of birds . . . and for this purpose constructed a device with bat-like wings". The framework was made of wood and rattan, and the wings, which spanned nearly forty feet, were covered with waterproof silk and controlled by three wooden levers, worked by the arms and legs. The tail, also covered with this strong silk, was twenty feet long.

De Groof first tried his invention out in Brussels, but when his attempt ended in complete failure he was banned by the authorities from any more such "foolhardy escapades". (It is interesting to note that the authorities throughout Europe were now giving a less free hand to those who wished to risk their lives in aeronautics: their examples were "not to the public good", as one French official put it after a ballooning accident.)

Not deterred, de Groof—now known as "The Flying Man", though he still was not—decided to try his luck in England. On 29th June 1874 he was taken aloft on the outskirts of the capital and released at 450 feet. With seemingly few problems, he glided down safely and landed in Epping Forest.

On 9th July he planned something much more sensational for the people of London. On that evening he ascended from the Cremorne Gardens under a balloon flown by a Mr Simmons. He rose up to 4,000 feet without mishap and then came down to approximately 1,000 feet above the Thames before releasing himself. This time, though, disaster struck: instead of bracing itself against the wind pressure, the wing frame streamed upwards as the "Flying Man" tried to get his levers operational and the whole contrivance crashed down into a street in Chelsea where de Groof was thrown out and killed instantly. The balloonist Simmons nearly met his death, for he drifted out of control for some time until he landed on a railway line in Essex right in front of a train. However, as a newspaper reported, "thanks to the almost superhuman exertions of the driver and guards, the train was brought to a standstill in time to avert a second fatality."

The following day *The Times* noted that this was the third fatality of a heavier-than-air machine and added that, "Such deplorable events as this serve to prove once more that the path of the inventor is indeed strewn with thorns".

If the newspaper could have seen a little ahead—or even been fully aware of the work another pioneer was doing at this time—it might well not have adopted such a pessimistic tone. For, hard on the heels of the development of the balloon, gliding flight was on the verge of being achieved: the endeavours of all those birdmen, tower jumpers, flappers, ornithopterists and others was about to be crowned by the work of the great German pioneer, Otto Lilienthal.

Lilienthal, who was born in 1848, has been called "The Father of Soaring Flight" and was undoubtedly the most important figure in aviation history in the last decade of the nineteenth century—if not one of the greatest men in the history of flight. He virtually created the art of motorless flight which was essential to the achievement of what we call mechanical flight—i.e. power-driven flight in an aeroplane—and his work led directly to the achievements of the Wright brothers. He did what no man before had done—keep aloft with fully convincing mastery and stability.

Lilienthal was a man of amazing mental ability linked to manual skill, and as a student at a Berlin technical college had shown early promise by obtaining the highest honours ever granted to a pupil at that seat of learning. With his brother Gustav, he became absorbed in the whole European attitude towards aerial investigation, and spent many hours studying the flight of birds, particularly that of the stork. Edgar B. Schieldrop in his *Conquest of the Air* (1957) has admirably described these early years:

> It may be said that Lilienthal first took the naive way towards flight. He fastened wings to his shoulders and tried to fly as Icarus had done in the myth. He began at the age of 14 with twin boards, which he fastened to his arms with straps. Naturally enough this did not work, but, unlike his predecessors, young Otto did not give up.
>
> He studied the masters of the art, the birds, but did not propose to beat with his wings, realizing that the movement was too complicated. A bird does not always beat its wings in flight; it sometimes glides, and it was this gliding flight that Lilienthal felt could be imitated by man. All birds' wings are arched—and he was without doubt the first man who fully realized the advantages of this form and studied it thoroughly.

The result of this study—and some halting experiments with ornithopters—was the publication in 1889 by Lilienthal of his *Der Vogelflug als Grundlage der Fliegekunst* (Bird Flight as the Basis of Aviation)—one of the classic works of aviation. The book was a compendium of twenty-five years of hard-won experience, and apart from dealing with the best shapes for wings, discussed the movement of the centre of pressure on them during flight, the problem of maintaining stability, and the question of the power required for flight.

But theory had never been enough for Lilienthal: he wanted passionately to fly himself, and in 1891 began experiments with gliders on the outskirts of Berlin. Here he built an artificial hill fifty feet high, and from this he would run forward into the wind, hanging beneath the wings. He has left us with a graphic description of how it felt to be the first man to master the air on wings:

With folded wings, you run against the wind and off the mountain, at the appropriate moment turning the bearing surface of the wings slightly upwards so that it is almost horizontal. Now, hovering in the wind, you try to put the apparatus into such a position in relation to the centre of gravity that it shoots rapidly away and drops as little as possible.

The essential thing is the proper regulation of the centre of gravity; he who will fly must be just as much the master of this as a cyclist is of his balance. Obviously, when one is in the air, there is not much time to ponder about whether the position of the wings is correct; their adjustment is entirely a matter of practice and experience.

Lilienthal went on:

After a few leaps, one gradually begins to feel that one is master of the situation; a feeling of safety replaces the initial fear. Hovering in the air, you no longer lose either calmness or self-possession, while the indescribable beauty and gentle sensation of gliding along over the expanse of sunlit mountain-slopes serves merely to increase one's ardour on each occasion.

It is not long before it is all one to the aviator whether he is soaring along six or forty feet above the ground; he feels with what certainty he is borne along by the air, even when the tiny people down below are peering anxiously upwards towards him. He travels over deep chasms and soars for several hundred yards through the air without the slightest danger, parrying the wind successfully at every moment.

Lilienthal's first gliders were single-winged and he was supported in the middle under the forearms by small bolsters which left his hips and legs free once he had taken off. These he used for control and stability, swinging his body forwards, backwards or sideways to shift the centre of gravity. He was sustained in the air by the wind, so naturally his most successful early flights were those made in a breeze.

H

Obviously these glides required much skill and practice to accomplish as M. J. B. Davy notes. "Lilienthal made hundreds of them covering distances of over 100 yards while descending at the rate of 1 in 7 or even less. He succeeded, however, in gliding nearly horizontally in winds of about 20 m.p.h. and in high wind he was sometimes lifted from the top of the hill without the necessity for running down it.

The result of these experiments was that he was able to study the behaviour of a supporting surface in the air and the rudiments of how it could be controlled. The experiments served also —and this was important—to create confidence in the idea of human flight and to inspire others to explore further; it was no longer a fantasy since Lilienthal had placed it upon a practical footing.

In 1893 Lilienthal adapted his 'hang-gliders', as one might describe them, giving them cambered wings with radiating ribs and a fixed rear fin and freely hinged tailplane to prevent the craft from nose-diving. With these modifications he achieved glides ranging from 300 to over 750 feet, and could exert considerable control over his craft.

By 1895 he had constructed a still more successful biplane glider, and was making take-offs from natural heights such as the Stollner Hills near Rhinow. In successive prototypes he began experimenting with a leading-edge flap device to counteract air pressure on the vaulted upper surfaces of the wings, as well as steering air brakes. He also invented a new form of body harness to enable his movements to control the craft more exactly.

The future achievements which loomed before the German at this moment in time seemed almost limitless. Indeed, he was on the verge of fulfilling another scheme in linking power to his glider in the form of a small gas motor to control the movements of the wing tips, when disaster overtook him.

On 9th August 1896, while testing this new device on the Stollner Hills, he crash-dived from a height of fifty feet. He was rushed to hospital with a broken spine, but the dedicated work of the doctors could not save him and he died the following day, aged 45. In five magnificent years he had made over a thousand pioneering glides.

Charles Gibbs-Smith pays a tribute to this aviator whose writings were so widely read and influential, and of whom

photographs—the first in the history of a man in flight—
brought home the actuality of flight to a world-wide audience:

It is hard to overestimate the vital force which this great
pioneer injected into aviation, as much after his tragic death as
before. His strange retention of a boyhood ambition, at a time
when petrol motors and propellers were clearly destined to be
used in flying machines, marks Lilienthal's historic position as
the culminator of the nineteenth century's efforts in practical
flying, as well as the precipitator of the conquering period to
come.

There were, of course, many imitators of Lilienthal once
he had succeeded. In Britain, a Scotsman named Percy Sinclair

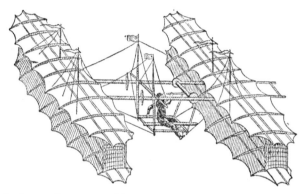

One of the rather more bizarre creations of Lilienthal's French
disciple Captain F. Ferber. This "Lamsonscher Flyer" was built in
1898 at Paris

Pilcher, who had made two visits to Berlin to watch Lilienthal
fly, developed his own 'hang-glider' along similar lines. Sadly,
he, too, was killed in his most advanced design, "The Hawk"
in 1896. He had already made glides of over 250 yards and
was on the verge of adding a light oil engine to his wings
when the accident occurred. His craft was distinguished by its
unique wheeled undercarriage and by the fact that it was
launched by a tow-line.

The main French 'pupil' of Lilienthal was an artillery officer,
Captain F. Ferber, who appears initially not to have progressed
further than constructing replicas of the German's earliest
gliders and flying them with only modest success, although

later, after the success of the Wright brothers, he played an important part in launching similar experiments in Europe.

It was in America, in fact, that Lilienthal's work was to be most successfully continued by the man who provided the final link in the chain with the Wright brothers. He was a civil engineer named Octave Chanute who, though born in Paris in 1832, went to the United States when he was six, and remained there for the rest of his life. Chanute is believed to have become interested in aviation after meeting the English pioneer, F. H. Wenham, and therafter collected all the available research and data which he summarized in another milestone work in the history of aviation, *Progress in Flying*, published in 1894. Following the death of Lilienthal, whom he greatly admired, Chanute took on the mantle of encouraging inventors via the press, and although he was already too old (at 64) to fly himself, began to build gliders, assisted by A. M. Herring, a former pupil of the German master.

Chanute set up a testing ground on the shores of Lake Michigan, near Chicago, and in the two years 1896–7 Herring made several flights in various machines before the partnership produced the now-classic two-surface 'hang-glider' with its advanced form of controls, support and tail unit which was to make over 700 flights.

Although, later, Chanute did make a few further experiments, he was by 1900 in close contact with two inspired and inspiring brothers, Orville and Wilbur Wright, and he subsequently became their confidant and closest friend. It was his advice and guidance, plus the inspiration the brothers had found from the work of Lilienthal, which was to lead to their success first in gliding and later in the ultimate achievement of powered flight.

When Chanute moved quietly from the centre of the stage —after being, perhaps, the most remarkable and productive 'middleman' in history, as one historian has called him—the Wright brothers at last opened the door in December 1903 for man to move when and where he chooses in the skies. Obviously, there is no call here to repeat the familiar details of the two brothers' work and achievements at Kitty Hawk.* It is, though, interesting before closing this section and moving

* I have, however, come across a fascinating letter by Wilbur Wright about his early endeavours and this is reprinted as Appendix II.

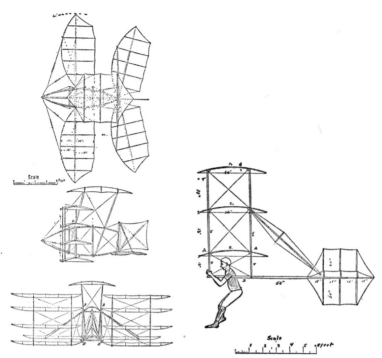

(left) Plans for the glider made by Octave Chanute
(right) A gliding machine made by Chanute in partnership with
A. M. Herring

on to the modern birdmen, the seekers after man-powered
flight and the exponents of hang-gliding, to note a prophetic
link between the Wright brothers and that eccentric rural
deliveryman about whom I wrote at the very beginning of
this book. He, as you will recall, made his ill-fated attempt to
fly in the small Essex village of Chigwell Row. The Wright
brothers, so the records indicate, were the descendants of a
lay-preacher named Samuel Wright who emigrated to Spring-
field, Massachusetts in 1636. And where had this worthy man
come from? Essex, England, where it is said part of his circuit
had included that small community of Chigwell Row. . . .

[10]

Man-Powered Flight Today

Since the achievement of sustained and controlled flight by the Wright brothers and the subsequent developments which have brought aviation into the modern jet age, the schemes and projects of the birdmen and man-powered flight enthusiasts have been a small and mainly slightly eccentric adjunct to aeronautical history. Man's intrepid spirit has, though, never accepted that flight under his own power is impossible, and from the turn of the century there has been a continuing stream of weird and wonderful machines built for this endeavour. However, until the formation of a special organization under the aegis of the British Royal Aeronautical Society in 1959 to document such attempts, reports are in the main fragmentary and hard to come by.

This is, of course, understandable: in a world making aeronautical progress in huge leaps and bounds, anyone who persisted with such ancient ideals as those of the birdmen ran the risk of being, at best, labelled a crank, and at worst, publicly ridiculed. Yet such is human nature that there were still those who tried; from the stories I have collected I have selected a number which are both typical of many more, and world-wide in range. I have also reproduced a number of cartoons from turn-of-the-century European periodicals which illustrate the general public attitude: one Italian example even shows men and birds having changed places in the order of things!

A story which is surely typical of dozens more from just about anywhere you care to name is that related by journalist Alexander Frater in an article he wrote recently on man-powered flight for the *Daily Telegraph*. He says:

An old acquaintance of mine named Pilgrim, whose life was a long and painful sequence of abortive schemes and missed opportunities, once turned his attentions to designing a machine for man-powered flight. It was christened the Stratoscooter and it consisted of three pram wheels and a kitchen chair flanked by tapering wheels and a pear-shaped paper fuselage, painted brown. The propeller was driven by pedals, leaving his hands free to work the controls. He built it in a Suffolk barn and, a week before the maiden flight was scheduled, a horse wandered in, evidently mistook it for a mare, and mounted it.

The damage was evidently repaired and, on a calm, summery evening, Pilgrim wheeled it out onto an empty road, climbed aboard and set off. He was just clear of the ground, pedalling hard, when an unexpected gust of wind lifted him to a height of thirty feet and he stalled. The Stratoscooter struck the wall of a mental hospital and broke up. Pilgrim, together with the wreckage of his dreams, was catapulted into the grounds of the establishment, where he landed, cursing, smack in the middle of a group of manic depressives sitting under an umbrella having tea. The plane was a write-off and so, in effect, was Pilgrim. He relinquished all further dreams of riches and esteem and went back to his job with the local bailiff, serving writs on a bicycle.

Mr Frater goes on to recall that it "seemed a hell of a joke at the time" as there is "something inherently droll about the pretensions of people trying to fly". Those who see nothing funny in the idea, he adds, "regard it as a kind of holy crusade and risk their necks in the attainment of a dream which has preoccupied man ever since he understood that the grip of gravity was permanent and uncompromising".

Another man of the same purpose as Mr Frater's appositely named "Pilgrim", though he could hardly have been farther away, was a Japanese, Chuhachi Ninimiya, who, around the turn of the century, built a series of man-powered contrivances. He is one specific example of just how universal the desire to fly was at this time, and though a model of one of his man-powered machines—shown elsewhere—indicates the potential of the idea, he apparently abandoned all his experimentation once word of the Wright brothers' success reached Japan. An Australian, Lawrence Hargrave, was also experimenting in a similar manner at this time, but seems to have devoted his major resources to kites and therein played a part in the development of the stable aeroplane. It has been claimed that if Hargraves had emigrated to Europe, instead of working in isolation, he would "undoubtedly have been able to absorb the contemporary moods and accomplishments, and progress to important attainments in aviation".

It is perhaps only to be expected that there was much frantic experimenting among Americans after the achievements of Orville and Wilbur: as a nation the people were flushed with pride, and inventors were anxious to claim other aeronautical laurels. A Californian, Professor Montgomery, tried to improve on the idea of the Belgian de Groof who launched himself from a balloon, and designed a glider-like machine which was taken aloft and then set free. In 1905, when the first trial was made, a friend of the professor, Dan Maloney, agreed to pilot the craft and after his release immediately achieved the distinction of being the first upside-down flyer in history! The glider had flipped over as soon as it was set free, but thanks to keeping a cool head, Maloney managed to coax the machine back the right way up and then drifted slowly down to earth.

On the opposite side of the country, in New York, another would-be conqueror of the air was experimenting with wings made of aluminium. Although the name of this man is lost— only a fading photograph survives—his use of a light metal in constructing the bird-shaped wings is one of the earliest records of its use. Over this frame was stretched a canvas covering and the machine was intended to be launched from an incline or hillside. I have been unable to trace any record as to whether it flew or not.

Perhaps the most fascinating of these American pioneers was the remarkable Major R. Franklin-Moore of Washington, D.C., who devoted his life to extraordinary aerial projects. He built gliders to imitate Lilienthal, aircraft to copy the Wright brothers, and wings to follow the birdmen. Sadly, for all this endeavour, Major Franklin-Moore achieved little success and scarcely any recognition: in my photograph he is posing with his "Flying Fox Wings"; a man was supposed to hang under them and manipulate them in a 'flapping' manner while controlling the direction by movements of his body.

The French were also, needless to say, sparing no effort in aeronautical experimentation: indeed, many people in the country were still smarting that they, who had first risen into the skies in a balloon, should have been beaten to the same achievement with wings by the Americans. One of their most adventurous schemes was the establishment of the Flying School at Lille where inventors and students alike could learn to fly gliders—launched by a tow-line—and hopefully pick up the expertise necessary to overhaul the lead of the Americans.

With man-powered flight still unattained, the combination of the bicycle and cambered wings seemed to several Frenchmen the possible solution. On many a French road in the first decade of the twentieth century, cyclists with wings affixed to their bikes—like that in my photograph—could be seen pedalling frantically along trying to take off. Exhaustion and bruising when they were toppled over were the sole attainments of most. A Parisian, Count de Guiseux, is said to have achieved modest hops with his "Aeroplane Bicycle" in which a propeller was linked to the drive chain of the back wheel and highly geared so that it turned at a much faster rate than the Count pedalled. Kite-shaped compartments in which the propeller was located were an obvious aid to lift when there was any kind of breeze.

In England, R. M. Balston of Mereworth in Kent made several experiments with a 'flapping-wing' aircraft in 1906–9. The first of these was to be moved by man-power, but despite the special gear-system, human stamina gave out before the contrivance could become airborne. Later, Balston linked the wings to a small petrol engine (the petrol engine had been developed in 1885 by Benz), but even the flapping that resulted from this power was of no use.

The British also tried pedal power in various forms, but there was probably no stranger craft than the "Rickman's Flying Machine" developed by an industrialist and his assistant. As my photograph shows, two cyclists endeavoured to whirl the umbrella-shaped lifting device fast enough to raise them from the ground. Predictably, they failed.

In Germany, too, men were seeking the freedom of the skies, like the unfortunate Herr Gross-Lichterfeld, who experimented with several sets of wings in Berlin at the turn of the century. His most determined attempts were to improve on the wings which had so nearly succeeded for the Swiss clockmaker, Joseph Degen. Tragically, when apparently near success, a jump from a high building in the German capital ended in disaster as one wing caught a balcony and man and machine plunged helplessly to the ground. Gross-Lichterfeld was dead before a doctor could reach him.

The invention of the aeroplane, had, of course, already opened up new possibilities in the field of war, and although the subject of aerial combat is of no concern in this book, it is interesting to find that the Germans were studying the possibility of man-powered flight both prior to and during the First World War. How seriously this was pursued it is difficult to tell: certainly a cartoon of the period, shown elsewhere, makes a joke of the whole idea. But the English and Italians also looked into the idea, both then and again later in World War II.

The Nazis actually offered a prize of 5,000 marks for the first man to achieve a flight of 550 yards under his own power. The only recorded attempt was by a Herr Duennbeill who tried but failed with a cycle-and-wings machine; he was, however, awarded the Reich Leader of Air Sport prize by Hermann Goering as compensation.

There is also a bizarre story told that Lord Beaverbrook, the newspaper magnate and friend of Winston Churchill, gave considerable financial backing in the early 1940s to an English inventor who was endeavouring to perfect a set of specially designed wings. The man apparently jumped off several hillsides, but had to abandon the scheme when he found the muscular strain so great that he twice broke his arms!

Turning back briefly in time, there were two very nearly successful man-powered flights in America in the inter-war years. In 1923 it was claimed there was a very short self-propelled flight by a cycle-plane, but as the inventors found the results far from encouraging, they abandoned the project there and then, and the details now seem far from conclusive. In 1937, however, an Italian immigrant named Enea Bossi did pedal himself into the air near New York and achieved what some experts claim was the first ever man-powered take-off (not flight, I must underline, but take-off). It was, though, a most positive start.

There were two other aircraft built in the 1930s for which limited flights were claimed, although experts remain sceptical. The ingenious plane built by the Haesller–Villinger partnership in Germany had 40-foot wings which could be rotated to catch the wind, but it had to launched by a bungee. The Italian Bossi–Bonomi "Pedaliante" was a much heavier and larger craft and similarly it is believed that the pilot's efforts had to be augmented by a mechanical lift-off.

The most important figure in the field at this time was Alexander Lippisch, who built several aircraft in Europe and was the first man to design and build a delta-wing aircraft as far back as 1930. In 1929 he also created a flapping-wing man-powered aircraft which, although it was not successful, showed his keen interest in such projects. (Now living in America, Lippisch has formed a group of like-minded enthusiasts who are experimenting with ultra-lightweight planes in Iowa.)

It was not until two decades after these hesitant attempts that man-powered flight began again in earnest. This time, though, there was to be an official body set up to supervise and record the attempts—and the incentive of a substantial prize for the first man to fly.

The Royal Aeronautical Society in London is the world's oldest aviation body and its influence international and authoritative. Founded in 1866 as simply the Aeronautical Society, it attracted inventor and scientist alike and, as we have seen in these pages, there was much discussion and experimentation about flight by the members long before it was achieved. Since the advent of flight, the society has played a leading role in supporting research, and numbers some of the world's most distinguished aeronauts in its ranks.

In April 1959, as a result of a sudden new upsurge of interest in the possibility of man-powered flight following informal meetings held by a group of enthusiasts, the RAeS was approached and urged that these endeavours should be put on an organized footing. Almost immediately it agreed to the establishment of a sub-group within the RAeS, to be called The Man-Powered Aircraft Group. Money to support the most likely projects was obviously a necessity, and the RAeS appealed to the government for aid. The request actually got as far as a discussion in the Houses of Parliament, but, seemingly, no one considered the idea quite sound enough for the expenditure of public money.

Hansard reports the amusing speeches of a number of MPs, including that of Mr L. W. B. Teeling, the member for Brighton

Pavilion, who proposed the motion for government aid. He said,

> There is a wonderful future for us. I can well imagine, because of traffic, my Hon Friend the Parliamentary Secretary and I taking off in order to get here. We would have to get only just over ten feet in the air, just above the buses . . . From my constituency point of view, I should like some of the tests to be made at our own Shoreham Airport, so that we could then go gaily along Brighton Front at top speed going from meeting to meeting. No doubt every Member of Parliament would get extra votes by being seen at such a height.

It was amusing, of course, but got the new group nowhere. However, throughout history, men who have set out to imitate the birds have not been easily deterred, and these new enthusiasts were no different. As the authoritative magazine *Flight* put it:

> The committee had no outside backing and no money. Nevertheless, it set about trying to make information available to interested people so that the problems could be clarified in the hope that, if man-powered flight did seem to be practicable after further study, someone would build an aircraft and prove that it could be done. . . . The MPAG held lectures and meetings to discuss the many problems of man-powered flight, while the committee worked hard to build up a fund to enable any promising design to be built, because it was realized that those likely to attempt such a project would have little money of their own.

Funds were not easy to come by, but then in November of that same year, the Man-Powered Aircraft Group had a sudden and unexpected benefactor: an industrialist, Mr Henry Kremer, who was a friend of one of the committee members, gave a substantial donation and offered to put up a prize of £5,000 for the first successful flight of a man-powered aircraft designed, built and flown within the British Commonwealth. The result, as one newspaper described it, was that "the country was swept by a power-it-yourself flying fever". The secretary of the Group was inundated with letters and telephone calls proposing schemes of all shades of probability. As the prize—which has twice been increased since 1959, to £10,000 in 1967 and a massive £50,000 in 1973, and is now open to anyone in the world—still awaits a winner, the reader may be interested in seeing the simple rules laid down by the Kremer Competition Committee:

The entrant, designer and pilot must be citizens of the United Kingdom or the British Commonwealth, and the aircraft must be designed, built and flown within the Commonwealth.*

The aircraft must be a heavier-than-air machine and must be powered and controlled by the crew over the entire flight. The use of lighter-than-air gases is prohibited and no devices for storing energy are permitted.

No limit is set to the number of crew.

Flights are to be made in still air, i.e. a wind not exceeding 10 knots, and from approximately level ground on a course to be approved by the Royal Aero Club, who are officially to observe each flight.

The course is to be a figure-of-eight with two turning points not less than half a mile apart. The starting line will also be the finishing line and will be between the turning points, approximately at right angles to the line joining the turning points.

The height, at both the start and finish of the course, must be not less than 10 feet above the ground.

The aircraft must be in continuous flight over the entire course.

The aircraft will be considered as gliders and no permit to fly or Certificate of Airworthiness will be required, but all entrants must be insured against third-party risks.

The Committee has stated that the design of the craft is entirely at the discretion of the inventor, although ideally it should be a conventional fixed wing plane, an ornithopter or something resembling a helicopter. With such an incentive, would-be birdmen everywhere took to their drawing-boards and workshops. Some of the earliest attempts on the groups' files are worth repeating for their ingenuity.

An RAF Warrant Officer, Spencer Bailey, of Melksham, Wilts, built a two-man cyclopter of mild-steel tube. The occupants pedalled a drive chain which whirled around a 20-foot rotor blade, and, hopefully, lifted it up into the air. When the machine was demonstrated at an RAF exhibition, it only managed to climb two inches from the ground. Unaware of the double meaning in his words, WO Bailey told onlookers

---

*Now no longer applicable, although there are special extra prizes for Commonwealth citizens.

he still had "a long way to go". He had indeed, for he was shortly afterwards posted to Aden.

A London sculptor, Emiel Hartman, managed at Cranfield to get his ornithopter a little higher, but serious damage to the machine's bird-like wings prevented further experiment. A Sheffield engineer, Alan Stewart, attracted a lot of attention to the small craft he built in his back garden. He had to lie underneath the machine and pedal a series of gears to launch it into the air. Unfortunately four years of effort were of no avail.

Another man from the north of England constructed a helicopter in his garage, but, sadly, when he tried to take it out for trials it proved too large for the doors and he had to dismantle it again. When he laid out the pieces on his lawn he found that for some reason he couldn't fit them back together again! In Scotland, a man built an ornithopter from barrel staves and heavy tape, but when he launched himself off a barn it crashed helplessly to the ground. "I think," he announced painfully from his hospital bed the next day, "it would go better with an engine."

In the Commonwealth the story was much the same. An engineer in Perth named Barry Ranford built a 350-pound aircraft with wingspan of 30 feet, which one unkind critic described as "looking like Moby Dick with wings". Despite energetic pedalling, the machine remained immovable.

In South Africa a Mr Sanderson Chirombo attempted to get airborne with a bicycle fitted with wings and a tailplane. Dressed somewhat bizarrely in a lounge suit, goggles and crash helmet, he pedalled furiously across an open stretch of land until, stricken with cramp and still firmly on the ground, he fell over. A Johannesburg bush pilot, 74-year-old Jack Vine had a little more luck when he managed to get his fixed-wing craft 20 feet into the air and covered a distance of nearly 200 yards. However, before he could get any further, a gust of wind tipped it over and smashed the wings. Mr Vine plans another machine with a propeller on the tail and has announce that he will "fly it to Cairo".

Canada also has its enthusiasts, and the Canadian Aeronautics and Space Institute has formed a Man-Powered Flight Section to encourage such work. Experiments have been going on under the direction of the glider designer, Waclaw Czerwinski, with special emphasis on studying the 'elastic' properties of bicycle-driven aircraft.

The rest of the world has not been lagging behind, and at least seventy groups of individuals from a dozen different countries have registered their intention of competing for the prize. The Japanese were early entrants, with Professor Hidemasa Kimura of Hihon University constructing four versions of his "Linnet", all of which have flown increasingly well, and Professor Eiji Nakamura presenting the blueprints of a multi-winged pedal-power craft, the 'Sato-Maeda OX-1'.

From Austria, Josef Malliga has entered his paper-covered pedal plane which weighs only 113 pounds empty and has a wingspan of 65 feet. It has already flown 150 metres at a height of one metre from a muscle-powered take-off, and over 400 metres when tow-launched.

A 76-year-old designer, Umberto Carnevali, leads the Italian birdmen, and has conducted extensive tests with his flying machine at Urbe Airport near Rome. Before the Kremer prize was thrown open to the world, Carnevali had indicated he might change his nationality so as not to be disqualified from claiming the reward.

After a comparatively indifferent beginning, the Americans have shown more enthusiasm of late and there are now several individuals and groups busy with projects. Plans have also been made to develop man-powered flight as a popular sport, with a national competition and prizes for the best constructions and performances.

The Northrop Institute of Technology in California has carried out some fascinating experiments in this field and also built an ultra-lightweight (70-pound) two-man pedal plane, the "Flycycle", which has an 80-foot wingspan. Recently, it became the first man-powered craft to fly in America, albeit very briefly. The students also came up with the interesting fact that because of the strain of simultaneously pedalling and controlling such an aircraft, an average physically fit man can only sustain an output of 0.3 to 0.5 horsepower for a few minutes. It therefore takes an airframe of high aerodynamic efficiency, extremely light weight and a large wingspan to fly on this minimum power.

In a nutshell, this is why man-powered flight is now seen as the pursuit of young, fit men, weighing around 150 pounds

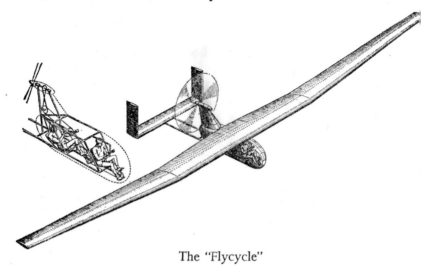

The "Flycycle"

and in a craft constructed not merely of the old staples like balsa-wood and paper, but fibre-glass, epoxy resin and expanded polystyrene: again of a total weight of 150 pounds. Because the craft are extremely cumbersome, they call for exact handling, and this has to be linked to great strength in turning the pedals which drive the rod or chain connected to the propeller. Such a combination of flying officer and professional cyclist is obviously not easy to come by.

The most industrious—and successful—pursuit of man-powered flight has undoubtedly been in Britain; as the *Daily Telegraph* reported last year:

> Our small but single-minded teams of enthusiasts have been labouring so assiduously that, today, we lead the field and, to emphasize that small but piquant achievement, we have the world record for distance under our belt.* The Man-Powered Aircraft Group is constantly receiving new applications for grants, though fifty per cent tend to come from cranks with preposterous and unworkable schemes.

* This record was set on 29th June 1972 by the Halton Man-Powered Aircraft Club's "Jupiter" which flew for 1,171 yards at RAF Benson in Oxfordshire. The aircraft was flown by Flight-Lieutenant John Potter at an average height of 12 feet and a speed of about 30 feet per second. The duration of the flight was 1 minute 47.4 seconds, and it was officially observed by the Royal Aeronautical Society and the United Service and Royal Aero Club. The previous best distance was 993 yards, set by John Wimpenny in 1962. Further details are given later in this chapter.

(*above*) The American birdman Clem Sohn showing his canvas wings before a flight. He died in April 1937 when his parachute failed to open. (*below*) The Frenchman Leo Valentin, who achieved flight with wooden wings after being dropped from an aeroplane. Here he is gliding to earth from 9,000 feet. He, too, died in an accident in 1956

(*above*) Bert Hansell fails to fly the River Nene at Peterborough in a machine built by the Branbridge Flying Club, Kent (1971). (*below*) This "flapping machine" built and piloted by M. L. Dolling of Swindon barely covered a few yards at the annual Birdman Contest at Selsey, Sussex

More scenes from the Birdman Contest of 1975 at Selsey: Rosemary Ogden, the 20-year-old psychology student and intrepid birdwoman. Like the men, she failed to make the 50-metre mark, but was beaten by only one other contestant

Chris Burrows in one of the most professionally produced machines seen at Selsey. Sadly, like all the other entrants so far, he had to be fished out of the sea in the end

Angels away! Stephen Crouch and Andrew Horner, perhaps the most bizarre of Selsey's birdmen, complete with haloes. Instead of striking heavenward, however, they plunged unceremoniously down into the sea

(*above*) David Cooke came closest to flying the 50-metre Selsey course. The 35-year-old Suffolk draughtsman hit the sea 5 metres short of the mark, but the judges ruled that he had also allowed three people to give him a helping push. (*below*). This unsuccessful but ingenious plane was the work of Commander Michael Collis, Chairman of HMS *Dolphin* Hang Gliding Club

The birdman as an advertising figure: three moments
from a popular Benson and Hedges TV commercial
with Julian Orchard as a birdman whose flight ends in
disaster, but who can console himself with a cigar

Front cover for Tom
Greer's fine novel about
an Irishman who learns
the secret of flight by
watching sea-birds. (*below*)
The very latest-style
birdman: Bud Cort
starring in *Brewster
McCloud*, directed by
Robert Altman for MGM
(1971)

A popular children's comic character, "Jim Solo the Birdman", who with his canvas wings took on criminals and evildoers of all kinds

(*above*) "The Flying Boy", another dedicated opponent of crime who flew through thousands of daring adventures and was an antecedent of Batman and Superman. (*left*) Perhaps the most famous of the American comic-strip heroes with birdman qualities, Batman, with his young assistant, Robin

Birdmen featured in the high adventure film *Darkest Africa*, produced by British Lion in the 1930s

A birdman utilized in a sophisticated advertisement for aviation training

Graduates...How about a career in flight simulation?

No, we're not suggesting that you try this kind of leap into the unknown. But it's a very real and important business designing, making and marketing Flight Simulators to help train the world's aviation men. Link-Miles of Lancing do just that, and need lively, quick-thinking graduates of all disciplines to help them do it.

Just a few facts: each Flight Simulator is a complex electro-mechanical device which simulates the cockpit, instrument panels, flight motions and audio visual events involved in flying a given type of aircraft in all imaginable conditions. There is instantaneous computerised control of all these variables. As a result, pilots can train safely, thoroughly, on the ground. We design each Simulator as a special 'one-off' project tailored to one type of aircraft. And we sell them all over the world.

Graduate opportunities

Being a happily middle-sized company employing about 800 people at present, we can be flexible in our approach to graduate intake and training. Basically we would want you to experience quickly the day-to-day realities of each sector of our business – Administration and Finance, Development and Production; Systems design, development and production – to discover where you best fit in. You'll get to know the work and problems of talented specialists in all these areas, in a friendly, stimulating atmosphere. We work hard and play hard, with the Sussex coast and Downs nearby.

Link-Miles
A DIVISION OF SINGER

Phone Brian Townson on Lancing 5881 and we'll arrange to show you around.

The Singer Co. (UK) Ltd., Link-Miles Division, Chartwell Road, Churchill Industrial Estate, Lancing, Sussex.

"It's his quiet confidence that impresses me"

KEVIN WOODCOCK

The birdman as an inspiration for cartoonists: (*left*) from the *News of the World*, 16th April 1972; (*below*) from *Punch*, 1975

"*Sometimes I feel he can be over-ambitious.*"

(*above*) A recent development by enthusiasts in America has been the biplane hang-glider which, though more difficult to launch than the kite, can be equally flexible and exciting in the air. (*below*) A hang-glider enthusiast almost hits a spectator as he lands after a flight in California

Up, up and away! Firmly settled on his seat, the enthusiast can climb and fall with his hang-glider as long as his inclination and the air currents will allow him to. (*top right*) Swinging from side to side to get his angle of ascent correctly adjusted, this enthusiast begins the exhilarating climb into the heavens. (*bottom right*) A safe landing. With the sun setting, a colleague assists the enthusiast to land by grabbing the back of the wing

(*left*) The joy of hang-gliding – birdman Alan Winsor of Benfleet in Essex takes off into the wide blue yonder. . . . (*below*) One of Europe's finest hang-gliding pilots, Yannis Thomas, takes off for another flight – a birdman in the style man has dreamed of for many centuries

Four major fixed-wing aircraft have emerged in Britain, all of which have flown, and it is worth mentioning them briefly. They are the Southampton University aircraft "Sumpac", the Hatfield "Puffin", the Halton "Jupiter", which holds the world record, and the two-seater "Toucan" from Hertfordshire.

The first machine to be completed and flown after the announcement of the Kremer prize was the 80-foot-wingspan "Sumpac", built by Southampton University students of spruce and balsa with a nylon covering. It took 4,000 hours to build and after extensive tests, was flown on 9th November 1961 at Lasham by gliding instructor Derek Piggott. It rose into the air about 5 feet and carried for more than 50 yards. Experts were understandably impressed by this flight—particularly as Piggott had no special cycling training—and with modifications the machine later achieved distances of up to 650 yards. It also took a small step towards Mr Kremer's figure-of-eight course by making limited turns of about 80 degrees.

Only a week later, the first rival to the "Sumpac" made its inaugural flight; this was the "Puffin", built by the thirty-five members of the Hatfield Man-Powered Aircraft Club. The members, all employees of the de Havilland aircraft factory, took thirteen months to build the machine, which was constructed of the familiar spruce and balsa but had 84-foot wings, on which for the first time a transparent plastic covering of Melinex sheet was used. The fuselage was also covered with this sheeting. The group had several advantages over is rivals in that it had the de Havilland facilities available to it and many of the component parts were given by aeronautical suppliers. But, as chairman John Wimpenny reported later, they had to work under conditions of strict security for they suspected that spies were afoot!

The machine was called "Puffin", said Wimpenny, "because of the puffin' it took to get it airborne." And that was just what the de Havilland test pilot Jim Phillips found when he gave it its first run on 16th November—yet he managed to keep it in the air for 30 seconds. The following year, anxious to prove that it was possible for anyone to fly the aircraft, John Wimpenny decided to fly it himself. Although he admitted to dieting and cycling the five miles to and from work each day in preparation, there was no denying the outstanding nature of his performance on 4th May 1962 when he pedalled "Puffin"

I

up to 8 feet and flew a distance of 993 yards in 2 minutes 1 second. The Royal Aeronautical Sociey's sub-group were so impressed that they awarded him a special £50 prize for being the first Briton ever to man-power a plane more than half a mile: and his record stood for exactly ten years.

The third of the single-seater aircraft is the much publicized "Jupiter", now in the charge of RAF apprentices at Halton. The machine is made of balsa and plastic wood and is covered with an ultra-lightweight skin of 'Mylar' plastic. It has a wing-span of 80 feet, a 9-foot propeller and weighs just 146 pounds when empty. It is perhaps strangely appropriate that we should find that this, the most successful of man-powered machines, began life in the garage of a young inventor named Christopher Roper in . . . Chigwell, Essex. Unable to get backing for his design from the Royal Aeronautical Society, Chris built the aircraft at his own expense, but had barely finished work when a fire broke out which virtually destroyed the machine. Knowing he could not go on himself, the young designer handed what was left of his creation to the team at Halton, who, after 10,000 man-hours, had it airworthy again.

On the bright, windless evening when the "Jupiter" snatched the world record from the "Puffin", it was piloted by Flight-Lieutenant John Potter who had previously flown Hunter jet fighters. Describing the achievement to the press as the "high point of my career", Potter added, "actually, I've done 1,200 yards before, but it couldn't classify for the world record as not all the required scrutineers were present."

From Flight-Lieutenant Potter we learned what it was like to be one of the first men in history to enjoy a sustained and controlled man-powered flight: the dream of every birdman, tower jumper and flapper since the time of Icarus. The attempt followed months of practice and training and was undertaken before official scrutineers on the runway (which is considered essential to give the 'pedal pilot' a firm surface) at RAF Benson.

Dressed in a track suit and suitably 'warmed-up' before entering his cockpit, Potter began pedalling with a man holding the end of each wing up; they let go when the ailerons became effective at 5 knots. At 8 knots the rudder was operational and a slight pressure on it to the right was needed to prevent torque from the 'human engine'; at 16 knots there was a sudden lift of the tail. Feeling this pull, Potter increased his steady cycling to the faster pace of 18 knots, and when he had covered just 150 yards from his start, touched his handle-bar controls and lifted the huge craft smoothly up into the air.

Still bearing down hard on the pedals, he adjusted the eleva-tors and climbed up to 25 feet, levelling back to 15 feet. A quick look down at the ground below through his sweat-covered windscreen, a glance at his instruments to satisfy himself he was at the correct cruising height, and he settled his pace to a steady 17.5 knots. The only sounds were his own breathing, the gentle whirring of the propeller, and the slight whoosh of the air outside. He felt in control, relaxed and con-fident. He was flying quite certainly by his own unaided power and skill.

For over a minute more he pedalled on, then through his opaque windscreen he saw houses and hedgerows begin to loom at the end of the runway. He did not yet have the ability to turn the machine and therefore had to land. Slowing his pace, he dropped gently down and, making a small nose-up adjustment and with a touch of rudder to bring the aircraft straight, he felt the bicycle wheel bump gently on the runway and then hold. He had beaten John Wimpenny's record by 200 yards and still felt "as fresh as a daisy".

The flight had also established a number of important facts, such as there being a very real danger of stalling the aircraft if it was taken above 25 feet, and that 21 mph was the best cruising speed. Above this figure, endurance is compromised by the excess effort needed, while below there is once again the risk of stalling. In essence, added Potter, man-powered flight is a combination of the bottom half of the pilot "pedal-ling like mad" to get airspeed, while the top is "making fine adjustments to the controls".

The fourth major operation has been undertaken by a team called the Hertfordshire Pedal Aeronauts, who believed, quite simply, that perhaps two men in a man-powered aircraft would succeed better than one. Their craft, the "Toucan", carries both a cyclist and a pilot. With a man to concentrate on each of the major requirements stressed by Potter (though the pilot is expected to pedal, too) the craft has, of necessity, got an enormous wingspan of 139 feet—which makes it just 6 feet shorter than that of a Boeing 707 and without question the largest man-powered aircraft in the world. The twenty-strong team which built the "Toucan" was led by an aeronautical lecturer, Martyn Pressnell, and it took 20,000 man hours and some £800 to complete before being launched in December 1972. It flew a very creditable 700 yards. (Another two-man aircraft, with the occupants sitting side by side, has been built by a group of thirty enthusiasts in Southend, Essex. It has a wingspan of 90 feet, but the propeller is placed in a somewhat unusual position, slightly ahead of and above the wing. So far it has only flown very briefly.)

All of these machines still have far to go to win Henry Kremer's prize—and, indeed, several entrants have already fallen by the wayside through accidents resulting in expensive and lengthy repairs (a tailplane, for instance, can contain as many as 12,000 individually cut and glued pieces) or their constructors' becoming involved in other projects. Some disillusioned entrants believe the figure-of-eight course is impossible for such machines. "It's like trying to turn a bicycle with an 80-foot pole lashed to the handlebars," said one member of the Hatfield group.

Nonetheless, work is going on, and those still involved—like the intrepid Flight Lieutenant Potter—believe the answer lies in aircraft with smaller wingspans. "We've done some theoretical work," he says, "limiting the size and wingspan of these aircraft which, at the moment, are very cumbersome and subject to the slightest wind. If, when turning one of the present craft, you inadvertently put too much bank on—say five or six degrees—you simply lose control. We think the new aircraft will be a great improvement. It will be built of sheets of glass fibre reinforced with carbon fibre, and with the right wingspan of about fifty feet, could get round the Kremer course in about six minutes. The actual flying will involve a series of large circles, taken very steadily, and by the time we have actually flown the mile course we will have covered a true distance of three or four miles."

The important American journal, *Practical Science* concurs with this view: "Man-powered aircraft of the future will be smaller, simpler, sturdier and cheaper than those built to date. A skycycle perhaps similar to that of Josef Malliga in Austria, but with a wingspan of about 50 feet, would be ideal for sports flying and an excellent student project."

The British magazine the *Pilot* also sees the sports potential of such aircraft and noted recently:

> The new thinking centres on studies of machines suitable for purely sporting purposes, rather than for direct attempts at the Kremer prize. The idea is to produce simple designs than can be produced by small groups with limited workshop facilities and that are easy to transport, assembled and rig. They must be robust both on the ground and in the air.
>
> Dr Keith Sherwin of the University of Liverpool, and one of the nation's leaders in the theory of man-powered flights,* has produced a basic specification for a sports machine with a span of not more than 50 feet (which alone would remove many problems) and which would fly at about ten feet above the ground, needing, he says, about 0·48 hp for the purpose. The height of the flight is related to the distance of the wing above the runway, as ground effect is very significant.
>
> A machine with this wider range of uses must be less critical in weather limitation, for only early morning or late evening flight in calm conditions has been possible until now. Dr Sherwin suggests that a wind of ten knots must be acceptable for the new-generation sporting type. Mini-thermals off hard runways could play their part, too, and vertical air movement of only one foot per second would be beneficial; this, he says, is possible at a height of ten feet with a temperature difference of only two degrees between the runway and the grass alongside it. The sporting design would have power to the propeller but none to the wheels, with six-degree diheral on the wings to dispense with the need for ailerons, and the fuselage would be of the pod and boom layout.

More than one cynic has suggested that all this recent frantic activity in man-powered flight on both sides of the Atlantic has not only to do with the Kremer prize, but the fact that those old villains of the peace, the Russians, are carrying out advanced studies into the possibilities. According to the reports, the Russian Association for Co-operation with the Airforce, Army and Navy is concentrating its energies not on bird-flight but the way insects fly. The capabilities of in-

---

* Dr Sherwin is the author of *Man-Powered Flight* (1972), widely regarded as the most authoritative work in the field. He has also constructed a sports skycycle, the "Liverpuffin", with his students, which has flown briefly in trials, and recently delivered the following resounding statement about man-powered flight: "The present state of the art is rather like the Wright brothers attempting to fly the Atlantic in 1903."

sects, they say, are far superior to birds, and they quote the highly sophisticated manœuvring and hovering of the dragon-fly and the lifting powers of bees. From this study, it is believed, the Russians will soon be producing an extraordinary man-powered machine which will take off and land anywhere, hover and even fly sideways—all by the power of human limbs!

It has to be said that nowadays it is not just the converted who believe that, eventually, everyone will be able to take to the air in cheap and simple 'bird machines'. In 1964, for example, the British Naturalists' Association issued a warning about the possible invasion of the countryside by man-powered skycycles, and urged that any such cases of trespass should be regarded as a criminal offence. Today more and more ordinary people are becoming involved in investigative schemes, seemingly unable to wait—in the words of one newspaper commenting on the BNA statement—"to get themselves arrested for pedalling their bicycles up and over the rooftops and into the wide blue vault of the sky."

In all seriousness, though, this continuing world-wide interest in man-powered flight is as hard to explain now as it was at the dawn of history. Certainly, the prize money is no answer. Aerodynamicists say that the research is valuable, and that even at this late date we may still find out something new about flying. Physiologists think that they might also learn something new about the capabilities of the human body.

The birdmen themselves put it quite simply: "The challenge is everything. While it's there to be conquered, there will be men who will try to conquer it."

Flight magazine summarized it most succinctly, I think, when a commentator wrote only recently:

The question is often asked: "What can man-powered flight achieve?" Apart from the fact that it has been one of man's ambitions since the days of Icarus, it is a challenge: something a man can achieve with his own personal skills. Perhaps there is no reasonable answer to the question. Man-powered flight is something which until recently had not quite been accomplished but which still had possibilities. It is that spirit which has dominated everything and everybody involved.

[11]

The Birdmen Hang on . . .

Apart from the man-powered aircraft, the birdman, pure and simple, still flaps intrepidly on. Although increasingly ridiculed by the public, there are still those who believe they can generate enough power to fly on aerodynamically constructed wings. Most have failed, but a few at least have known the soaring freedom which a bird enjoys—the incentive which fired the very earliest would-be flyer—when they have been dropped from aircraft.

Two names dominate the varied ranks of twentieth-century birdmen, the brave and ill-fated American Clem Sohn and the painstaking French enthusiast Leo Valentin. Both men achieved flight on specially constructed wings, having been dropped from planes and completing their descents on parachutes.

Sohn, whose enthusiasm for flight was fired by the exploits of Lilienthal and his fellow-countrymen, the Wright brothers, believed that it would be possible for a man to fly with wings if he had a parachute which he could employ to control his landing. To this end he designed canvas webbed wings which fitted from his arms to his legs, while between his legs he had an auxiliary sheet of canvas to act as a tail.

His initial experiments were carried out in America, where he jumped from a light plane and, once free, spread his arms and legs and performed limited gliding manœuvres. At the appropriate height he released the parachute strapped to his chest and descended to the ground. To raise money for more elaborate tests, Sohn embarked on a series of exhibition 'flights' in America, England and Europe.

Tragically, death awaited him when he appeared at a flying meeting at Vincennes, France, in April 1937. He jumped from 9,000 feet with his canvas wings and, according to eye-witness reports, glided down without any apparent problems to 1,800 feet. But this time when he pulled the ripcord of his parachute, the auxiliary canvas between his legs somehow got entangled in the unfurling parachute and caused it to stream upwards unopened. (The aeronautical term for this is 'Roman-candled'.) Even the reserve parachute could not break out of this tangle, and the helpless Sohn plunged down to a horrible death.

Shortly after this tragedy, a legend grew up that the first man from the crowd at Vincennes to reach the broken body of Sohn was the local 'birdman', Leo Valentin. In his biography *Homme Oiseau* (1955) Valentin dispelled this rumour by say-ing that he was not even present at the meeting—although he did learn a major lesson from the disaster which was to make his own later efforts much more safe:

> Had he possessed a sufficiently good free-drop and delayed-opening technique, Clem Sohn would have been able to save his life twice that day. For my part, I knew that I had mastered this technique. Thanks to my position I did not risk fouling the opening of the canopy and I knew what precautions to take to prevent the reserve parachute from 'candling' with the main one. In the realm of pure parachuting technique I had no qualms, at least as few qualms as one can expect in this profession. All that remained was to perfect the apparatus in as simple as possible a form to allow me to transform my free drop into flight. . . . Wings, but what kind of wings?

Valentin, who like Sohn, had been interested in flight since his childhood, undertook his research with painstaking thoroughness. He believed there were at least two basic faults in Sohn's canvas wings: the wings between the arms and legs were rigid, thereby making it difficult to control the release of the parachute, and the 'tail' was difficult to balance. To this end he used extra-pliant whalebones as the framework of his wings, and introduced vents into both the wings and the tail to help maintain the balance.

His early jumps were not the successes he hoped for: he still found control of the wings extremely difficult, and be-cause of the height from which he fell and the speed, the crowds who assembled to see the "Flying Man"—as he was billed—only caught a glimpse of him at the last moment, and many were convinced he was a fake! Soon after, Valentin became certain that canvas wings were just not the answer to this kind of flight, and although he made numerous further jumps throughout Europe which reassured both press and public that he was genuine, he secretly began developing new 9-foot wings of aerodynamically shaped wood hinged to a steel tube framework for his body. The apparatus weighed a total of 28 pounds as opposed to the 5 pounds of the canvas wings.

Again, Valentin encountered problems with the control of these new wings, but aided by a French aeronautical designer, M. Collignon, he changed their angle and balance, and by May 1954 was ready to make the most crucial 'flight' of his life from the airfield of Gisy-les-Nobles near Sens. Accompanied by his assistants, he took off in a DC3 just before five o'clock on a fine, warm afternoon. In his own words, this is what happened:

The DC3 completed the last turn. We were at 9,000 feet. It flew eastwards. I went over to the wide door which had been fixed up in the port side of the fuselage. The time had come . . . woods, fields, villages . . . I jumped.

The moment the pilot banked to the left I jumped with closed wings, facing the tail. In the slipstream I found myself on my back with my wings open. I had just time to catch a glimpse of the photographer leaning out of the fuselage, and then . . . nothing more. I was alone in the sky. I rounded my back. In a dive I rolled over onto my stomach. Then began a series of close turns to the right. Using my arms, I stopped this spiral and for a few seconds glided very correctly on an even keel.

This time there was no mistake . . . I was gliding. I was flying! I felt myself floating on air as in a glider. Then a spiral began to the left. It had nothing in common with the spin I had experienced on previous occasions. Merely a series of close turns. This spiral was probably due to the excessive dihedral formed by the wings. That must be rectified later.

I turned over on my back. I flew best and with most stability in this position. Something else to study. I rolled over again face downwards.

Another spiral. I was already at 3,000 feet and I had just crossed the last line of wooded country separating me from the airfield. I pulled the ripcord. It opened without a hitch. I undid the corset and released the wings. . . . I landed at the extreme north of the airfield in a field of lucerne.

By the time my friends arrived in a jeep I was already out of the harness and had taken off my helmet and glasses. "Bravo, you've done it!" they cried. "You've really flown this time!" Yes, I had flown, in fact I was the first man to have flown. Bird Man now meant something.

To all intents and purposes, Leo Valentin had flown like a bird for more than three miles. After 1954, he flew again on several occasions, attempting to perfect both the construction of his 'wings' and the technique of flying them. But, as he had said, much remains to be done, for "Today is still the dawn of the first day of the lone man in the sky".*

The success of Valentin, and to a degree that of Clem Sohn, undoubtedly gave birdmen everywhere a much appreciated fillip, and in 1974 they were offered a carrot not unlike that dangled before the man-powered enthusiasts by Henry Kremer: an anonymous donor put up a £1,000 prize for the first "birdcraft" to fly the English Channel.

The donor had lodged the money with the British Light Aviation Centre as an encouragement to "oscillatory propulsion". The rules allow the craft to be lifted into the air by machine power, but it must be propelled forward by flapping wings like those of a bird.

An annual gathering of birdmen is also now being held at Selsey on the Sussex coast each August to compete for a £3,000 prize which is offered for the first birdman to fly 50 yards under his own power.

The enthusiasts have to leap from a raised platform on the lifeboat station catwalk and endeavour to pass a marker 50 yards away in the sea. Lifeboatmen are on hand to pull the unsuccessful from the water!

Since its inauguration in 1971—when the first prize was £1,000—the competition has attracted a variety of contestants: some bizarre, like teenager Christopher Hemery, who simply glued hundreds of hens' feathers to his arms and chest (shades of Icarus!); intrepid like a nineteen-year-old student, Rosemary Ogden, who got further than most of the men by

---

* Leo Valentin also met his death while demonstrating his wings, in May 1956. He was appearing at a charity airshow at Liverpool Airport before a crowd estimated at 100,000 people. Valentin made his usual jump from his Dakota aircraft at 8,000 feet, but almost immediately complications developed with his wings and he crash-landed. He died later the same day from extensive head injuries, aged 37.

gliding 30 feet; and some determined, like physical-training instructor Peter Fry, who fell only 10 feet short of the prize on his hang-glider.

America, too, has its yearly gathering of birdmen in May at Newport Beach, California, overlooking the Pacific. This function, professionally organized and publicized through a newsletter for enthusiasts called *Low and Slow*, attracts contrivances of all kinds—wings, gliders, *et al*. A prize, the Otto Lilienthal Memorial, is presented for the best overall performance, and to date has never failed to be awarded for a glide of less than 800 feet.

Of course, there are still lone enthusiasts like those tower jumpers and birdmen of early times, who take off from the heights and fall with undaunted belief. Men like Walter Cornelius, who tried to fly over the River Nene at Peterborough in England. Cornelius—no relation of the William Cornelius who designed a manually operated ornithopter with a foot-operated tail in 1884—tried to clear the river with 10-foot wings by leaping from the roof of a supermarket close to the water's edge. Unfortunately for this professional strongman, the elastic in his wings broke and he fell straight into the water. He said afterwards he felt he would need bigger wings for any further attempts.

Or Donald Partridge, who jumped from Hammersmith Bridge in London wearing a single wing made of cloth, wood and feathers. He hoped to fly to the next bridge, but instead fell fifty feet into the water below. Dragged quickly from the water, he told a waiting journalist, "I feel akin to the birds. As you can see, I am called the partridge, and my first name is Donald, the same as that of the famous duck".

Such attempts sound rather silly, of course, and ignore the fact we have established in these pages that man's body unaided is not strong enough to lift him into the air to fly. Man's heart alone provides a basic problem—it represents only 0.5 per cent of his total weight, whereas that of the golden eagle is over 8 per cent and that of the tiny humming bird up to 22 per cent. The heart also only normally beats at a rate of 70 times a minute, while even the common sparrow's throbs at an amazing 800 times a minute when in flight. As John W. R. Taylor has observed, "These are essential features of a bird's high-revving engine, and a man would need a six-foot

chest to hold all the muscles he would need to fly, even if his
body had wings."

All the same, our fascination with the idea of flying like
the birds will surely endure as it has done since the earliest
times. The birdman is, after all, always there to remind us
of his intent—a recurring theme in our literature, a staple of
children's comics and cartoonists' jokes, not to mention a
figure in art, sculpture, music, advertising and films. He flies
on as ever in our dreams, on our televisions and radios, and
even through our day-to-day conversations. We should surely
miss him deeply if he were not there.

It would be wrong, I think, to conclude this book without some
mention of the new activity of hang-gliding, it being the
natural extension of Lilienthal's momentous pioneer aviation
work, and the most accessible and practical way for the
ordinary man or woman to experience what nearly amounts
to man-powered flight. (I exclude gliding from mention here,
as it is really a separate adjunct of aviation history, and the
planes themselves of course require launching by machines or
aircraft.)

Hang-gliding is a new sport, a thrilling and exhilirating one
which, it has to be underlined, can be dangerous for the un-
trained: it has already claimed more than two dozen lives in
America and about half that number in Europe, not to mention
injuring many exponents of varying degrees of skill. The craft
can take off from a small hillock or dune, or the top of a hill
or cliff, and the flight success, at speeds varying between 15
and 20 mph, depends on a mixture of riding the wind and
careful manœuvring.

Hang-gliding—or 'sky-surfing' as it is sometimes called—
began in America in 1970, although the creation which made
it all possible had been evolved in 1951 by a National Aeronautics and Space Administration (NASA) scientist, Francis
M. Rogallo. Rogallo had been employed on a multi-million-
dollar research project to find a replacement for the parachutes that lower spacecraft to the earth's surface after they
have returned to the atmosphere. His solution was a form of
kite with a flexible delta wing, which was deployed, and had
its shape maintained, by a series of tension lines—in much

the same way as the shape of a parachute is maintained by its shroud lines.

Although the kite was subsequently felt by NASA to be unsuitable for its intended purpose and the project was dropped—primarily because it was difficult to stow and deploy —a number of people interested in aerodynamics quickly conceived modifications that would convert the craft into a serviceable 'hang-glider'. One of these was a Massachusetts aerospace engineer named Michael Markowski who was particularly impressed by the kite's glide-ratio of four in one, which meant that the craft only dropped about one foot while travelling well over four.

Markowski therefore substituted an airframe of tubular aluminium for some of the tension lines of the Rogallo kite and fitted the structure with a control bar in the form of an inverted Y. He also added a harness which suspended the pilot in a sitting or prone position as desired, and from which he could hold the control bar and exert the necessary force on it to move it in any direction. His sail consisted of Dacron sailcloth and the total weight of the craft was 40 pounds. Thus was the prototype hang-glider born.

After making a number of experimental craft, Markowski developed what he believed to be the best version, and took it to the ideally suitable winds of Southern California— almost literally learning the art of hang-gliding by trial and error. Later, in the highly regarded journal *Scientific American*, he produced the first guidelines for the new activity:

> Sky-surfing is an art. It can be mastered only by diligent practice. The Rogallo kite can be flown almost anywhere that suitably sloped terrain faces the prevailing wind. The novice is urged to begin his training at the foot of a small grass-covered hill or sand dune with a slope of about 25 degrees. There should be a steady, uphill breeze of about 10 miles per hour. Be certain that the breeze is free of gusts that might dump you or abruptly lift you 20 feet or more.
>
> When you have assembled the kite near the bottom of the slope, put it down with its nose in contact with the ground and pointed directly into the wind. When you have inspected the glider and checked that everything is in order, grasp the upright members of the control frame, lift the kite above you and run forward with the nose pointed directly into the wind. As you run, tip the nose alternately upwards and downward at increasing

angles to sense the effect. Raising the nose will cause the sails to inflate, catch more wind and pull upward, thereby reducing the speed at which you can run. Lowering the nose has the reverse effect; it decreases the wind resistance and enables you to run faster.

Markowski goes on to the method of take-off:

Continue practising on level ground until you can unerringly predict and feel exactly how the wing will react to every angle at which you will hold the kite. Then strap yourself into the harness. Continue practising on level ground until the harness feels natural.

At this stage you can begin to work your way up the slope. At first, however, go up to an elevation of only two or three feet. *Always point the nose of the kite directly into the wind*, even when you carry the kite uphill. As you gain proficiency, the wind will even help you carry the craft up the slope. When you run downhill, hold the control frame near the bottom, so that the uprights pass close to your shoulders.

Finally, from an elevation of 10 or 12 feet, begin running downhill with the sail barely inflated. As you pick up speed, push the control frame away from you somewhat, thus pitching the nose upward. If you have reached sufficient speed, you and the kite will rise into the air. If not, your forward motion will simply be retarded. In that case keep trying until you acquire the correct combination of forward speed and pitch angle for flight. Soon you will be skimming the ground.

Now, says Markowski, the real test begins.

Once you have become airborne, maintain your fore-and-aft balance by shifting your weight. Push against the control bar to move your weight backwards, which will increase the angle of pitch and thus reduce your speed. Pull the bar to shift your weight forwards, thus decreasing the angle of pitch and increasing your airspeed. Shift to the right by exerting lateral force on the control bar to make a right turn, and do the opposite for a left turn.

Remember, when you are sky-surfing only two or three feet above the surface, it is better to err on the side of keeping the nose high and flying too slow than to pull the nose down sharply, which will make the craft dive and expose you to the risk of hitting the ground harder than you would like. Continue practising near the base of the slope until ground-skimming becomes second nature. Then work your way gradually to the summit.

Concentrate first on learning to maintain fore-and-aft balance, that is, pitch. If your craft starts drifting sideways, slow down and land as quickly as possible to avoid being blown into the side of the slope. As you gain skill in maintaining balance in pitch, begin to practise turns. Your first turns should be gentle, smooth and wide. Shift your weight by pressing sideways on the control bar very gently.

All turns cause the kite to sink at a faster rate than when it flies in a straight line. You can compensate for this tendency somewhat by increasing the angle of pitch slightly during the turn. Avoid pushing the nose up to the angle at which the glider would stall, lose flying speed and drop towards the ground. The optimum angle of pitch can be sensed only with experience.

Finally, says the scientist, by way of advice:

As you begin to progress to higher altitudes you will have occasion to make sharper turns and to manœuvre in the three dimensions of space, but do not rush your learning process. Word has somehow spread that the Rogallo kite is an exceptionally safe craft. In actuality it is only relatively safe. Aerodynamically the wing is characterized by a very gentle stall, meaning that when the kite begins to lose flying speed, it tends to settle rapidly and to nose down slowly instead of going abruptly into a nose-dive. Its performance is governed by the same laws of physics that affect other flying machines.

Almost as an afterthought, Markowski explained that to bring the kite into a gentle landing, the control frame had to be pushed right forward, thus bringing the nose up and causing the sail to act as an air brake. Experience had also taught him that it was a good idea to begin running in the air before touching the ground so as to avoid any jarring of the legs or spine when contact was made.

With this mastery of the hang-glider, Markowski was able to summarize the overall effect and encapsulate the feelings that were soon to make it an internationally popular sport: "It is an astonishing sensation to run along the ground for a few steps and rise effortlessly into the air. I scarcely realized that I was attached to a kite, because the craft represents only twenty per cent of the gross weight of the pilot-glider system. Suspended prone beneath the glider, the pilot has a sensation of consummate freedom, perhaps because of his bird's-eye view of the terrain."

By 1970, a growing number of enthusiasts were skimming their own versions of the hang-glider along the sloping beaches of the American west coast, or inland on hills, ski-slopes and even sand dunes. Some stuck with variations of the original Rogallo design, while others experimented with more traditionally shaped, single-wing and biplane gliders. Socially conscious observers were quick to see the attraction of the sport in ecological terms: there was no heavy machinery required and no polluting the atmosphere. Others thought it was because it was inexpensive (a glider of bamboo struts and a plastic wing made up by the owner could cost as little as $50) and it provided new thrills for the jaded surfers and motorbike riders. For a while, hardly anyone thought it might just be another variation of man's eternal desire to fly!

In any event, the Southern Californian Hang-Gliding Association swiftly came into being, followed by the introduction of safety measures including making it compulsory for the pilot to wear a harness and a crash helmet. Also magazines began to spring up with delightful titles like the *Sky Surfer*, *Ground Skimmer* and *True Flight*, which gives itself the grandiose subtitle 'The Bible real Birdmen have been waiting for'!

With the ensuing spread of the craze across America, a national organization was not long in being created, the United States Hang-Gliding Association. Apart from providing a central clearing-point for information on equipment, manufacturers, and the best places to experience hang-gliding, the Association found itself acting as mediator between the traditional school of glider enthusiasts with their expensive planes and control on their activities by the Federal Aviation Administration, and the freebooting 'sky-surfers' with their inexpensive craft who required no authority, and could launch virtually anywhere. As *Time* magazine reported in November, 1973:

Some sailplane pilots would sooner see hang-gliding go the way of pigsticking and jousting. Alvin Owens, vice president of San Diego's Decision Science, Inc, bristles at the mere mention of it. "It's a step backwards," says Owens. "I think it's extremely unfortunate for people to think about soaring and hang-gliding in the same context. It's like comparing the Soap Box Derby to the Indianapolis 500." The feud is particularly sharp at Torrey Pines, where all hands compete for precious airspace in one of the country's best known updrafts. Even the most adamant partisans, however, seem willing to glide and let glide in the common pursuit of lift.

The Association has, of late, been concentrating it efforts on emphasizing to people that proper training and skill are required to fly hang-gliders, as it is naturally anxious not to see any more deaths or serious injuries occur—events which, it believes, would cause some local authorities to ban the sport. It is not quite sure that the appearance of James Bond on a hang-glider in a recent film has presented the craft in its correct light to the public, but it certainly underlined the fact that the sport had arrived in a big way!

It was not long, of course, before hang-gliding had found its new disciples in Britain, and two organizations brought the various factions together: The British Hang-Gliding Association and the British Kite-Soaring Association. Like their American counterparts, they act as information centres for equipment and for advice about where to go for instruction, and publish regular newsletters. Membership of the BHGA also includes the useful advantage of a third-party insurance policy which provides compensation for any innocent bystander the hang-glider pilot might happen to hit!*

In England, the sport has drawn an enthusiastic press, despite a number of unhappy accidents. Colin Dryden in the *Daily Telegraph* in January 1975 enthused after trying it out: "Hang-gliding is quiet and non-polluting, relying on nothing but the fresh air of high places and the genius of Rogallo's nylon sail and aluminium tubing. It opens magic casements for the flyer while providing beauty for the spectator as sail wings swoop gracefully against the sky and hillside like so many great butterflies."

The sport is also fast catching on in Europe, with clubs burgeoning in France, Germany, Austria, Italy and Switzerland. Also, 'down under' in Australia and New Zealand.

In the Swiss Alps another version of the sport has been developed by a ski instructor, Konrad Freund, who has been teaching enthusiasts to fly their gliders with the aid of skis. The idea is simplicity itself: the hang-glider pilot skis with his craft up to a suitable point, then simply launches himself into the air, holding onto the control bar, of course. (Not to fall

* A full list of addresses of the major international hang-gliding organizations is given in Appendix IV.

K

behind in the search for new variations, the Americans have recently come up with 'flyking'—in essence, hiking with a hang-glider. Its proponents simply hang-glide from mountain-top to valley bottom, then climb up the next mountain and repeat the process, travelling as far as they choose—or as long as the mountains last.)

Like any other development in aviation history, hang-gliding —be it on Rogallo kite or ordinary wing—has found its new breed of heroes. Men like Robert Willis, an American who jumped off a cliff-face in Hawaii in October 1973 and remained aloft for the world-record time of 8 hours 30 minutes. (According to reports it was not weather conditions which ended his glide, but general fatigue and boredom!) Or Willis's fellow-countryman, Bill Bennett, who has been flying hang-gliders almost longer than anyone else, and apart from traversing Death Valley in Colorado, has the unique distinction of having been arrested for flying around the Statue of Liberty in New York. It was not so much the flight that upset the authorities, but the fact he landed on a stretch of grass where walking was prohibited.

In Europe, a Greek named Yannis Thomas has been responsible for some important variations to the Rogallo kite, and has made flights from mountainsides as well as with motor and vehicle-assisted take-offs. His most publicized flight was on 14th July 1972, when he tried to take advantage of the national holiday in Paris to fly under the Arc de Triomphe. Before he could complete his glide, however, he was stopped by the Police, as all winged contrivances have been banned in the vicinity since 1956. He has, though, flown around the Eiffel Tower several times, and emulated his great ancestor, Icarus, by flying over much of Greece, including the city of Athens.

The British champion is Ken Messenger, who has made some remarkable glides, including a three-mile soar from the top of Snowdon in 1973. In January 1975 he made a world-record flight in his Rogallo kite, being released from a balloon at a height of 12,700 feet over Newbury in Berkshire and descending safely to the ground.

The most important of all these intrepid birdmen is probably an Australian, Bill Moyes, a designer and inventor of great skill and ingenuity, not to mention personal courage. Towed behind a speedboat, he has climbed to 4,700 feet, and he has glided down the 12,349 feet from the top of New Zealand's Mount Cook. (This stood as the world record until Ken Messenger's descent.)

Hang-gliding, with its wonderful offer of the freedom of the skies in much the way that birdmen have dreamed throughout history, makes a fitting conclusion to our story. There are already plans for further developments in this field to make the craft safer, easier to handle and able to fly for longer distances. Some enthusiasts even want to add a drive system and propeller, while there are dreams of a self-launching sailplane with a pedal-driven propeller.

At long last, it would seem, we have reached the moment when man can look at the birds still with admiration, but with rather less of a sense of inferiority. For we can now fly, not perfectly, perhaps, or in their style, but with a sense of control, freedom and enjoyment—and only a minimum of danger if we do not take risks.

The dream of Icarus has finally been realized.

Appendices

I MAN AND THE BIRDS

An extract by Professor S. P. Langley, Secretary of the Smithsonian Institution, from his article "The New Flying-Machine" published in the *Strand* magazine, 1897.

Here is a human skeleton, and here one of a bird, drawn to the same scale. Apparently, Nature made one out of the other, or both out of some common type, and the closer we look, the more curious the likeness appears.

Here is a wing from a soaring bird, here the same wing stripped of its feathers, and here the bones of a human arm on the same scale. Now, on comparing them, we can see still

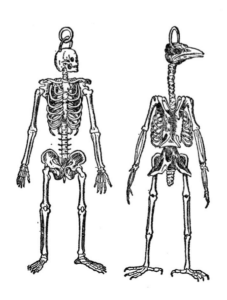

more clearly than in the skeleton, that the bird's wing has developed out of something like our own arm. First comes the humerus, or principal bone of the upper arm, which is in the wing also. Next we see that the forearm of the bird repeats the radius and ulna, or two bones of our own forearm, while our wrist and finger-bones are modified in the bird to carry the feathers, but are still there.

To make man, then, Nature appears to have taken what material she had in stock, so to speak, and developed it into something that would do. It was all that Nature had to work on, and she has done wonderfully well with such unpromising material; but anyone can see that our arms would not be the best things to make flying-machines out of. . . .

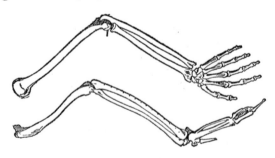

II MY INTEREST IN FLIGHT BY WILBUR WRIGHT

A letter received on 30th May 1899 by Professor S. P. Langley of the Smithsonian Institution, from a 32-year-old aeronautical enthusiast.

I have been interested in the problem of mechanical and human flight ever since as a boy I constructed a number of bats of various sizes after the style of Cayley's and Penaud's machines. My observations since have only convinced me more firmly that human flight is possible and practicable. It is only a question of knowledge and skill just as in all aerobatic feats. Birds are the most perfectly trained gymnasts in the world and are specially well fitted for their work, and it may be that man will never equal them, but no one who has watched a bird chasing an insect or another bird can doubt that feats are performed which require three or four times the effort required in ordinary flight. I believe that simple flight at least is possible to man and that the experiments and investigations of a large number of independent workers will result in the accumulation of information and knowledge and skill which will finally lead to accomplished flight.

I am about to begin a systematic study of the subject in preparation for practical work to which I expect to devote what time I can spare from my regular business. I wish to obtain such papers as the Smithsonian Institute has published on this subject, and if possible a list of other works in print in the English language. I am an enthusiast, but not a crank in the sense that I have some pet theories as to the proper construction of a flying machine. I wish to avail myself of all that is already known and then if possible add my mite to help on the future worker who will attain final success.

Yours truly,
Wilbur Wright

III FLIGHT BY 'BAT WINGS'

An extract from Benvenuto Cellini's autobiography in which he describes an experience in 1538 when he discussed flight with a mad Castellan who was keeping him a prisoner. It is one of the few mentions of flight by 'bat wings' in literature or history.

The Castellan had every year certain attacks of illness that entirely turned his brain; and when this attack began to come on he talked a great deal in a sort of babbling fashion; and these delusions were different every year: for upon one occasion it seemed to him that he was a jar of oil; another time it seemed to him that he was dead, and they must needs bury him; thus every year there came upon him some one of these different delusions.

This time he began by imagining that he was a bat, and whilst he was out walking he sometimes used to scream just as softly as bats do. He also made a kind of movement with his hands and his body as if he desired to fly. His doctors when they perceived it, as well as his old servants, afforded him all the pleasures that they could think of; and since it seemed to them that he took great pleasure in hearing me talk, they came constantly for me and took me to him. Wherefore this poor man sometimes kept me four or five whole hours, wherein I never ceased from talking with him. He kept me opposite him at his table to eat, and he never left off talking or making me talk; but during these conversations I used to eat very excellently. The poor man neither ate nor slept, in such a way that he tired me out, so that I could do no more; and looking him sometimes in the face, I saw that the balls of his eyes were full of terror, for one looked in one direction and the other in another.

He began by asking me if I had ever had the fancy to fly; to which I replied, that all those things that were most difficult for men I had most gladly sought to do and had done; and as to this subject of flying, since the god of nature had given me a body very fitted and strong for running and leaping, much more than the common run, with that small amount of skill beyond, which I should employ with my hands, I felt assured of the courage to fly. This man began to question me as to the means that I would adopt: to which I replied that having observed the animals which fly, and being desirous of imitating by art that which they had by nature, there was none that I could imitate except the bat. When this poor man heard that name of 'bat', which was the delusion under which he was labouring that year, he gave a very loud shout, saying: "He speaks the truth; he speaks the truth. This is the thing; this is the thing:" and then he turned to me and said, "Benvenuto! If anyone gave you the conveniences, would you also have the courage to fly?" To which I replied that if he was willing to give me my freedom afterwards, I had sufficient courage to fly as far as Prati making myself a pair of wings of waxed Rheims linen.

Thereupon he said, "And I too would have enough courage; but the Pope has commanded me to keep guard over you as if over my own eyes, and I know that you are an ingenious devil who would escape: however I will have you shut in with a hundred keys, so that you do not escape me". I set myself to beseeching him, reminding him that I was able to fly, but that out of the respect for the pledge that I had given him I had never failed him; moreover for the love of God, and on account of the many kindnesses which he had shown me that he would not add a greater misfortune to that great trouble which I was already enduring. Whilst I was saying these words, he gave express orders that they should bind me and take me to a well-secured prison. When I saw that there was no other remedy, I said to him, in the presence of all his attendants: "Secure me well and guard me well, for I shall certainly escape."*

IV ADDRESSES OF THE INTERNATIONAL HANG-GLIDING ASSOCIATIONS

These addresses were correct at the time of going to press.

Great Britain
The British Hang-Gliding Association, 'Monksilver', Taunton, Somerset.
The British Kite-Soaring Association, 8a, Rickman Close, Woodley, Reading, Berkshire.

United States of America
United States Hang-Gliding Association, Box 66306, Los Angeles, California 90066.
Self-Soar Association, Box 1860, Santa Monica, California 90406.

Australia
Australian Self-Soar Association, Frank Bailey, 42 Lansdowne Parade, Oatley, New South Wales 2223.

New Zealand
The New Zealand Hang-Gliding Association, Murray Sargisson, 14 Bean Place, Mount Wellington, Auckland.

* In fact, Cellini does later escape, but by the more orthodox method of stealing a key!—Author.

France
Fédération Français Vol Libre (FFVL) Philippe Galy, 29 Rue de Sèvres, 75006 Paris.

V FIRST SUCCESSFUL PEDAL POWER FLIGHT

A report by Reuters from the *Daily Telegraph* of 23rd April, 1976

A home-made, pedal-powered plane was flown one foot above the ground for 30 yards by Joe Zino, 52, a retired American Air Force pilot, at North Kingstown, Rhode Island, yesterday in what was believed to be the first successful flight in the United States of an aircraft powered by human effort.

Index